# Doug Jones

# Understanding the HEALING POWER

### of

# GOD

*HowTo Get it and What To Do
With It Once You've Got It*

Unless otherwise indicated, all Scripture quotations in this volume are from the *King James Version* of the Bible.

Second Edition
Second Printing 2002

ISBN 0-89276-964-5

In the U.S. write:
Kenneth Hagin Ministries
P.O. Box 50126
Tulsa, OK 74150-0126
1-888-28Faith
www.rhema.org

In Canada write:
Kenneth Hagin Ministries
P.O. Box 335, Station D
Etobicoke (Toronto), Ontario
Canada, M9A 4X3

# Contents

For the past twenty years, I have used the method of the laying on of hands to minister to those in the Body of Christ who were being oppressed by sickness and disease. This method is one that Jesus commissioned the Church to use in the sixteenth chapter of the Gospel of Mark, verses fifteen through eighteen.

Many have testified that they've actually felt the healing power of God go into their bodies. Yet you speak to some of the very same people three months later, and most of them are still very much bound by the same sickness and disease. There didn't seem to be any effects from the healing power that was administered to them through the laying on of hands.

As I searched the Word for answers, I discovered that there was one main reason why they were not being affected by the healing power that had been administered to their bodies. The reason was clear: It was the result of a lack of knowledge. As I continued to study, I discovered that there were two main areas that the sick lacked knowledge in. The *first* area is the lack of knowledge that when hands are laid on them, the healing power of God is *at that moment* administered to their bodies. This knowledge alone will make being prayed for in a prayer line so much more valuable and precious.

The *second* area is the lack of knowledge as to what to do with the healing power of God once it has been obtained. We have been giving people the healing power of God through the laying on of hands, but then we've been guilty of not instructing them as to what they are to do with it once they have obtained it. A lack of knowledge in this area is one reason why people have mishandled and mistreated the healing power of God.

Therefore, once we are ministered to by the laying on of hands, we must understand that there are laws that govern the healing power of God. Understanding these laws and cooperating with them will bring about the healing of our bodies that we have so longed for. Failure to understand and cooperate with these laws will cause us to remain as we are — bound by sickness.

Volumes of books have been written about faith and the role it must be allowed to play in our lives, not only to obtain healing, but also to live and walk by faith. As knowledge has increased, our confidence in and cooperation with faith has increased and has been strengthened. Similarly, this book is dedicated to bringing an understanding of *the healing power of God*. The more we understand this power, the better equipped we are to have confidence in it and the better able we are to cooperate with it.

The laws that you will be reading about in the chapters ahead will speak not only of how to obtain the healing power of God, but also what to do with it once it has been obtained. I encourage you to read all the scripture references carefully, even though they may be very familiar verses.

It is my prayer that as the eyes of your understanding become enlightened concerning the healing power of God, you will begin to cooperate with that power until your body is set totally free from the intimidating control of sickness or disease.

# 1
chapter

## The Team
## That
## Conquers
## Sickness

LUKE 5:17-26

17 And it came to pass on a certain day, as he [Jesus] was
   teaching, that there were Pharisees and doctors of the law
   sitting by, which were come out of every town of Galilee,
   and Judaea, and Jerusalem: and the power of the Lord
   was present to heal them.

18 And, behold, men brought in a bed a man which was
   taken with a palsy: and they sought means to bring him
   in, and to lay him before him.

19 And when they could not find by what way they might
   bring him in because of the multitude, they went upon the
   housetop, and let him down through the tiling with his
   couch into the midst before Jesus.

20 And when he saw their faith, he said unto him, Man, thy
   sins are forgiven thee.

21 And the scribes and the Pharisees began to reason, saying, Who is this which speaketh blasphemies? Who can forgive sins, but God alone?

22 But when Jesus perceived their thoughts, he answering said unto them, What reason ye in your hearts?

23 Whether is easier, to say, Thy sins be forgiven thee; or to say, Rise up and walk?

24 But that ye may know that the Son of man hath power upon earth to forgive sins, (he said unto the sick of the palsy,) I say unto thee, Arise, and take up thy couch, and go into thine house.

25 And immediately he rose up before them, and took up that whereon he lay, and departed to his own house, glorifying God.

26 And they were all amazed, and they glorified God, and were filled with fear, saying, We have seen strange things to day.

This story has been a favorite of mine for years. I have marveled at the determination of these men in verses 18 and 19, who tried every possible means of entering into this room where Jesus was. Can you imagine how they must have felt when they were not allowed into the room due to the crowd? Most people would have stopped there, turned around, and gone home. But it is very apparent that these men knew that help for their friend was in that room! They knew this yoke of palsy would be destroyed if only they could get their friend to Jesus.

Suddenly, one of the men has an unconventional idea: "Let's climb up onto the roof, cut a hole in the roof, and lower him into the midst before Jesus!" Agreeing with the idea, the men maneuver their friend onto the roof and begin their task of getting him to Jesus.

The first sign of their presence to those already in the room must have been the dust that began floating down from the ceiling. Then little pieces of the ceiling must have begun to fall on those below. Finally, a little bigger piece comes crashing down! All eyes at this time are looking upward.

The determined men continue to work. Now larger pieces are being taken off the roof until the men create a hole large enough to lower through it a man lying on a couch! As they lowered their dear friend through the hole, they must have been quite a sight. Covered with dirt and dust from the roof, all of them working together lowered him down to Jesus.

Verse 20 tells us of Jesus' reaction to this very unusual sight. It says, "And when he saw their faith, he said unto him, Man, thy sins are forgiven thee."

For years I have been so captivated by the statement *"And when he saw their faith. . ."* that it was the only thing I'd mention from this story. I had come to the conclusion that the only thing involved with this man's healing was their faith. But after reading this account a little more closely, I discovered that there were two things present which worked together to free this man from his disease. Luke informs us in verse 20 that not only was faith present, but in verse 17, he mentions something else that was present: *". . .and the POWER OF THE LORD was present to heal them."*

### The Unbeatable Team

What was this power that was present? It must have been *healing* power due to the fact that it healed the man! Therefore, we must come to the conclusion that this man's healing was the result of two things working together — *faith* and *the healing power of God!* This combination knows no failure. There is not a sickness known to man that can remain dominant in a person when faith and the healing power of God team up and work together!

Faith and God's healing power worked together to free this man from his disease. Then why had I spent so much of my time and effort defining and explaining the "faith" side while hardly mentioning the "power" side? If faith and power must work together as a team, we must understand as much about the power side as we do about the faith side.

Please do not misunderstand me. We must be taught about the faith side. However, if faith and power are a team, then we must know about each team member equally. We should not be elevating one above the other. If faith were the only thing responsible for the man's healing in Luke 5, there would have been no need to let him down through the roof. Those men had faith long before they lowered him into the midst before Jesus. So faith alone did not get this man healed; neither did the power alone get this man healed. It was the two working together.

When *our* faith teams up with *His* power, recovery from sickness and disease begins! This is the team that conquers sickness — faith and the healing power of God!

If we think about this account in Luke 5 for a moment, something very interesting begins to surface. There was only one thing in those men's lives that kept their faith from teaming up with the healing power of God, and that was the roof. If the team of faith and power was to unite and work together, the roof had to go! We see clearly that those men did not let a little roof stand between them and the healing power of God. It took a little time and effort, but the obstacle was removed. The team of faith and power was then united, and the sickness was conquered!

I wonder if we have anything standing between *our* faith and *His* power? I believe most of us do, and it must be identified and "ripped apart" if we expect to be free from sickness in our body.

### Another Example of Uniting Faith With the Power

In the Gospel of Mark, we have another illustration that helps us see the same point that was made in the previous story. It's the account of the woman with the issue of blood.

MARK 5:25-34

25 And a certain woman, which had an issue of blood twelve years,

26 And had suffered many things of many physicians, and had spent all that she had, and was nothing bettered, but rather grew worse,

27 When she had heard of Jesus, came in the press behind, and touched his garment.

28 For she said, If I may touch but his clothes, I shall be whole.

29 And straightway the fountain of her blood was dried up; and she felt in her body that she was healed of that plague.

30 And Jesus, immediately knowing in himself that virtue had gone out of him, turned him about in the press, and said, Who touched my clothes?

31 And his disciples said unto him, Thou seest the multitude thronging thee, and sayest thou, Who touched me?

32 And he looked round about to see her that had done this thing.

33 But the woman fearing and trembling, knowing what was done in her, came and fell down before him, and told him all the truth.

34 And he said unto her, Daughter, thy faith hath made thee whole; go in peace, and be whole of thy plague.

Reading of this woman's healing, it is very apparent that she has suffered much during the last twelve years before the time of her healing. She has spent all that she had trying to dethrone this disease in her body. She has endured many unsuccessful procedures by doctors to try to turn her situation around.

Suddenly, someone comes into this woman's presence who begins to tell her about Jesus. What wonderful news this must have been to her ears! A new possibility of being free becomes available if she can only get to Jesus! Immediately, she sets out to find this Jesus, and making her way determinedly, she finds Him. But as she evaluates the situation, she finds that a crowd has gathered, making access to Jesus almost impossible.

*We are lacking in knowledge concerning the healing power. We do not understand how to come into contact with it, how to obtain it, and what we are to do with it once it has been administered to our bodies.*

The woman undoubtedly had the thought cross her mind, *I'm not strong enough to push my way through that crowd.* Can you blame her for thinking that thought, knowing that she had been under that sickness for twelve solid years? For an instant, she no doubt must have entertained the notion, *Turn around and go home.* Then, suddenly, the words of her friend who'd told her about Jesus flash across her mind. And with renewed strength, she begins making her way through the crowd.

The closer the woman gets to Jesus, the thicker the crowd becomes. Her body is screaming at her, *You're too weak! You're never going to make it!* So to keep herself from yielding to those thoughts, she begins to say, *If I may touch but His clothes, I shall be whole.* Over and over, she says it as she makes her way through the throng.

Finally, the moment came, and she reached out as far as she could and touched Jesus' clothes. Immediately, Jesus turned around and asked His disciples, "Who touched Me?" As the disciples responded to the question, this little lady fell down before Him and told Him all the truth as to why she touched Him and what happened when she did (Mark 5:30-33). After hearing her wonderful testimony, Jesus says to her, ". . .*Daughter, thy faith hath made thee whole; go in peace, and be whole of thy plague*" (v. 34).

Here again, I do not know why I did it, but those words ". . .*thy faith hath made thee whole*. . ." captured my attention, and I thought of nothing else in connection with this woman's healing. Over and over, I would say and think about the words of Jesus: ". . .*thy FAITH hath made thee whole*. . . ." Once again, I had come to the conclusion that the only thing involved in this woman's healing was her faith. Therefore, for years, the only thing I taught on was the faith side. I'd never considered verse 30: "*And Jesus, immediately knowing in himself that VIRTUE* [or power] *had gone out of him*. . . ." But then I saw the team again. It was her faith and His power — His healing power —

that became united, and the sickness that had ruled her life for twelve years was finally defeated!

For too long we have majored only on the faith side. But we must remember that faith is only one member of the two-member team that conquered this woman's disease. It's time we became acquainted with the other member of the healing team — the healing power of God!

## Obstacles Will Try To Stand in Your Way of God's Power

Before we begin to learn about God's healing power, I find it interesting to note that this woman in Mark 5 had something in common with the man in Luke 5 who was lowered through the roof. The common "ingredient" was that she also had an obstacle between her faith and His power. In her case, the obstacle was a crowd. Had she not made her way through this crowd, the sickness would have never been destroyed. The man with the palsy had a roof between his faith and the healing power of God. Had his friends not ripped the roof off, so to speak, his infirmity would have remained.

Today you may not have a crowd between your faith and the healing power of God. You may not have a roof between your faith and the healing power of God. But most of us do have something between our faith and God's healing power, and that is a lack of knowledge. We are lacking in knowledge concerning the healing power. We do not understand how to come into contact with it, how to obtain it, and what we are to do with it once it has been administered to our bodies.

In Hosea we are told that ignorance will cause us to be destroyed. In Isaiah we are told that ignorance will cause us to become captive. We are being held captive and are being destroyed because of our lack of knowledge concerning the healing power of God. Ignorance concerning this second member of the healing team has been a reason many have failed to become free from their infirmities.

### HOSEA 4:6

6 My people are DESTROYED for LACK OF KNOWLEDGE: because thou hast rejected knowledge, I will also reject thee, that thou shalt be no priest to me: seeing thou hast forgotten the law of thy God, I will also forget thy children.

### ISAIAH 5:13

13 Therefore my people are GONE INTO CAPTIVITY, because THEY HAVE NO KNOWLEDGE: and their honourable men are famished, and their multitude dried up with thirst.

I will never forget a little lady who attended one of my services. As I spoke with her, she made a statement that I will never allow myself to forget. She said, "I refuse to be destroyed because I don't *know*." I have thought of that statement often, and it has made a tremendous impact upon my life. May we all have the same determination.

As you continue to read this book, I trust that it will clear a path for you "through the crowd" to put your faith in contact with the healing power of God. The chapters ahead will tear off for you the roof that stands between your faith and the healing power of God! But this book cannot make you walk through the crowd and touch the power for yourself; it cannot force you to lower yourself into the midst before Jesus. Only you can make that choice. I trust this book will encourage, inspire, and strengthen you to never stop until you have united your faith with His power. Remember, this team never loses!

# 2
chapter

# The Yoke Shall Be Destroyed Because of the Anointing

**ISAIAH 10:27**

27 And it shall come to pass in that day, that his burden shall be taken away from off thy shoulder, and his yoke from off thy neck, and the yoke shall be destroyed because of the anointing.

As I was teaching the Word one particular week, the Lord said to me, "I want you to study Isaiah 10:27." Now you must understand that at that time, I had been in the ministry for twenty years; yet I had failed to arrive at a clear understanding of what this verse was really all about. But as I studied Isaiah 10:27, it became very apparent that this verse provides tremendous hope to all who are bound by sickness and disease.

In order to understand this verse, we must look at and define two words: "yoke" and "anointing." If the yoke is going to be destroyed because of the anointing, then we must know exactly what is going to *be* destroyed and what is going to *do* the destroying.

### Defining the Yoke

In Isaiah 10:27 we are told that the yoke will be destroyed. Yet if we are unsure as to what the yoke is, then how will we know when it is destroyed? What is the meaning of this word "yoke"? The word "yoke" is used three different ways in the Bible:

**1) Literal sense.** When this word "yoke" is used in the literal sense, it speaks of a harness that connects two animals to a plow or similar farm tool. A yoke may connect two mules or oxen to a plow.

I do not believe that this is the type of yoke spoken of in Isaiah 10:27. Nowhere in the Bible do you find an illustration of the anointing destroying a yoke off of two oxen, allowing them to roam free! God has not given us the anointing for the purpose of destroying farm tools.

**2) Figurative sense.** Jesus used the word "yoke" figuratively in His teachings in Matthew.

#### MATTHEW 11:28-30

28 Come unto me, all ye that labour and are heavy laden, and I will give you rest.

29 Take my yoke upon you, and learn of me; for I am meek and lowly in heart: and ye shall find rest unto your souls.

30 For my yoke is easy, and my burden is light.

Here Jesus uses the word "yoke" figuratively. He took a phrase from the Jewish rabbis and incorporated it into His teaching. The Jewish rabbis had a saying that when you put yourself under a teacher — when you become a student of a particular teacher or when you willingly learn from a teacher — then you have taken upon yourself the *yoke* of the teacher. So when Jesus said, *"Take my yoke upon you. . . ,"* He is encouraging us to become His students. In other words, Jesus is saying, "Become a pupil of mine; become a student of mine."

You can see clearly that this is exactly what Jesus is saying when you read verse 29 entirely: *"Take my yoke upon you, AND LEARN OF ME; for I am meek and lowly in heart: and ye shall find rest unto your souls."* If you are a learner, student, or disciple of the Lord's, you have His yoke upon you.

In these verses, Jesus is *encouraging* us to take upon ourselves His yoke. If He is encouraging us to do this, then this type of yoke could not possibly be the type of yoke spoken of in Isaiah 10:27. God would never encourage us to take upon ourselves something that He intended to destroy off of us. God has not given us the anointing to destroy students or learners of the Lord!

3) **Symbolic sense.** In Isaiah 10:27, the word "yoke" is used in the symbolic sense. When the word "yoke" is used in its symbolic sense, it becomes a symbol of burdens and oppression. Anything that burdens or oppresses your life can and should be referred to as a yoke. By reading this scripture in its entirety, it is very evident that Isaiah was telling us that the anointing will free us from the things that burden or oppress us.

## ISAIAH 10:27

27 And it shall come to pass in that day, that his BURDEN
shall be taken away from off thy shoulder, and his
YOKE from off thy neck, and THE YOKE SHALL BE
DESTROYED because of the anointing.

Anything that burdens your body — anything that oppresses
your body — is a yoke. There is not a single thing in this life
that can burden your physical body or oppress you physically
that the anointing cannot free you from! This is wonderful
news, especially when we understand that oppression is a word
that is often used in the Bible to describe the effects of sickness
and disease.

## ACTS 10:38

38 How God anointed Jesus of Nazareth with the Holy
Ghost and with power: who went about doing good,
and healing all that were OPPRESSED of the devil; for
God was with him.

According to this verse, sickness and disease are classified as
oppression. The word "oppression" means *to exercise hard control over.* Sickness oppresses or, in other words, exercises hard
control over you by telling you where to spend your money,
when to go to work, and what you can and cannot do with
your family. Sickness and disease are an awful taskmaster! But
the Bible reveals to us that the anointing will free us from the
oppression of sickness!

Notice the phrase in Isaiah 10:27 that says, *". . .and the
yoke shall be destroyed because of the anointing."* This verse

did not say "the yoke *might be* destroyed because of the anointing." It said "the yoke *shall be* destroyed because of the anointing"! This word "shall" informs us that there is not a sickness that can attach itself to your body that the anointing cannot free you from. Glory! The anointing is disease's worst enemy! There is not a disease known to man that can withstand the anointing! There is not a cancer that the anointing cannot destroy. There is not a disease that we can inherit that the anointing cannot drive out of our body.

Oh, how this truth needs to be shouted from the house tops! Once this truth is understood, it will set us free from the worries and fears of what the doctors may say. No matter what name they put on the disease, we know that ". . .*the yoke shall be destroyed because of the anointing*" (Isa. 10:27)!

Now I don't know about you, but if I am being oppressed by sickness, and I discover that the only way out is through the anointing, then I am going to do everything within my power to learn how to obtain this anointing and how to cooperate with it to gain my freedom.

By way of illustration, if my employer came into my office and said to me, "Doug, you're an excellent employee; you are doing a wonderful job. But if you do not learn algebra, you can no longer work here." If my job depended on learning algebra, then every free moment I had, I would be studying algebra. Why? Because my job depends on it! My kids might come in and say, "Dad, do you want to go with us to the mall?" I would have to say, "No, not right now." Why? Because at *this* time, I must give my complete attention to learning algebra, because my job depends on it.

So if our life depends on the anointing in order to be free from the sickness that oppresses our body, then it would behoove us to do everything within our power to learn what the anointing is, how to obtain it, and how to cooperate with it. Therefore, we must begin by asking the question, "What is the anointing?"

## Defining the Anointing

Remember I said concerning Isaiah 10:27 that if we are to understand this verse, we must define the words "yoke" and "anointing." We now understand that the word "yoke" is a symbol of anything that would burden or oppress us. But what about this word "anointing"? In order to receive a clear understanding of this word, we must look for things in the Bible that freed people from oppressive yokes. When we see people being freed from the yoke of sickness, if we look carefully enough, we will find the anointing.

Let's examine three examples of Jesus ministering to the sick with the anointing. I believe these examples will give us a clear understanding as to what this anointing is. Remember, ". . .*the yoke shall be destroyed because of the anointing.*"

## The Anointing and the Sick Multitude

In Luke 6:17-19 we see the first example that gives us a clear picture of the anointing destroying the yoke of sickness and disease.

### LUKE 6:17-19

**17 And he [Jesus] came down with them, and stood in the plain, and the company of his disciples, and a great mul-**

titude of people out of all Judaea and Jerusalem, and from the sea coast of Tyre and Sidon, which came to hear him, and to be healed of their diseases;

18 And they that were vexed with unclean spirits: and they were healed.

19 And the whole multitude sought to touch him: for there went virtue out of him, and healed them all.

These people were being oppressed by sickness, but notice what freed them from their sicknesses. The answer is found in verse 19: *"And the whole multitude sought to touch him: for there went VIRTUE out of him, and healed them all."*

It was this "virtue" that flowed out of Jesus which destroyed their yokes. This virtue did the exact same thing that Isaiah said the anointing would do. It freed them from the sicknesses that burdened and oppressed their lives. So it appears by merit of its action and effect that this virtue is synonymous with the anointing spoken of in Isaiah 10:27.

Exactly what is this virtue that flowed out of Jesus? The word "virtue" means *power*. Then what kind of power was this that flowed out of Him? It must have been *healing* power due to the fact that it healed "them all" (v. 19)! So we could come to the conclusion that what will free *us* from sickness is virtue or the healing power of God or *the anointing*!

### Virtue, Power, and Anointing Are Synonymous Terms

These three terms — *virtue, the healing power of God*, and *the anointing* — are all the same thing when we are speaking of healing. Luke 6:19 says, *"And the whole multitude sought to touch him: for there went VIRTUE out of him, and healed them all.*" Notice that it did not say, "for there went *an anointing* out of Him." Why? Because the anointing and virtue are the same thing. The terms anointing, virtue, and the healing power of God are speaking of the same thing.

Many times while observing the sick being prayed for in church services, we will hear the ministers say, "That anointing went right into you; that power went right into you." They use the words "anointing" and "power" interchangeably.

Therefore, when we read Isaiah 10:27, "*And it shall come to pass in that day, that his burden shall be taken away from off thy shoulder, and his yoke from off thy neck, and the yoke shall be destroyed because of the ANOINTING,*" we could replace the word "anointing" with the word "virtue." We could even replace the word "anointing" with the phrase "the healing power of God." We could read the last phrase of this verse, "and the yoke shall be destroyed because of *the healing power of God*"!

(I must make you aware of the fact that this book is only talking about healing. We must not allow ourselves to think every time we see the word "anointing" that it is specifically speaking of the healing power of God. There is an anointing to teach, to preach, and so forth. However, we must remember that the product or result of the anointing is always freedom.

I have personally sat under men who were anointed to teach, and their teaching freed me from the yoke or oppression of false beliefs and false doctrine. False doctrine and false beliefs are as much a yoke as sickness is. They will exercise hard control over your life to the same degree that sickness will. False doctrine and false beliefs will destroy your life in the same way that sickness and disease will. Thank God for the anointing!

However, this book is dedicated to bringing an understanding concerning the anointing to *heal*. Therefore, I will limit my comments to the anointing that heals or, in other words, to the healing power of God.)

## The Anointing and the Woman With the Issue of Blood

Another example that illustrates the anointing destroying the yoke of sickness is found in Mark 5:25-34. It is the story of the woman with the issue of blood.

### MARK 5:25-34

25 And a certain woman, which had an issue of blood twelve years,

26 And had suffered many things of many physicians, and had spent all that she had, and was nothing bettered, but rather grew worse,

27 When she had heard of Jesus, came in the press behind, and touched his garment.

28 For she said, If I may touch but his clothes, I shall be whole.

29 And straightway the fountain of her blood was dried up; and she felt in her body that she was healed of that plague.

30 And Jesus, immediately knowing in himself that virtue had gone out of him, turned him about in the press, and said, Who touched my clothes?

31 And his disciples said unto him, Thou seest the multitude thronging thee, and sayest thou, Who touched me?

32 And he looked round about to see her that had done this thing.

33 But the woman fearing and trembling, knowing what was done in her, came and fell down before him, and told him all the truth.

34 And he said unto her, Daughter, thy faith hath made thee whole; go in peace, and be whole of thy plague.

Here in verses 25 and 26, we find an excellent description of the bondage of sickness and how it can oppress a person. This woman's sickness had exercised hard control over her for twelve long years. Think about how weak she must have been!

> *The anointing that destroyed the yoke of sickness in her life was the healing power of God!*

Think about how worried she must have been about her future, knowing that she had spent all that she had trying to get better.

Not only must this woman fight sickness, but she is also struggling against poverty. Yet notice that the instant she touched Jesus, something was transmitted from Him to her that freed her from this oppression. This "something" is found in verse 30. It says, *"And Jesus, immediately knowing in himself that VIRTUE had gone out of him, turned him about in the press, and said, Who touched my clothes?"*

When the woman touched Jesus, it says that "virtue" went out of Him and flowed into her. This virtue destroyed her yoke. This virtue destroyed the sickness that had burdened her life. What was this virtue that flowed out of Jesus? As I said before, the word "virtue" means *power*. What kind of power was this that flowed out of Jesus? It must have been *healing power* due to the fact that it healed her! The anointing that destroyed the yoke of sickness in her life was the healing power of God! So it appears once again by merit of its action and effect that this virtue or healing power is synonymous with the anointing spoken of in Isaiah 10:27. The anointing that will destroy the yoke of sickness in your body is the healing power of God!

## The Anointing Frees Another Who Is Oppressed by Sickness

A third example of the anointing freeing someone from the yoke of sickness is found in Luke 5. These three examples will help us obtain a clear picture that the anointing is synonymous with the healing power of God.

### LUKE 5:17

17 **And it came to pass on a certain day, as he [Jesus] was teaching, that there were Pharisees and doctors of the law sitting by, which were come out of every town of Galilee, and Judaea, and Jerusalem: AND THE POWER OF THE LORD WAS PRESENT TO HEAL THEM.**

Notice it did not say "and the *anointing* of the Lord was present to heal them." It used the word "power." What was the power of the Lord present to do? *Heal* them.

Do you see in this verse that, once again, the instrument that was used in the ministry of Jesus to free the sick is referred to as the "power of the Lord"? The yoke of sickness shall be destroyed because of the healing power of God or, in other words, the *anointing*! Jesus used the healing power of God to free people from sickness and disease. Once again, by merit of its action and effect, this power is synonymous with the anointing spoken of in Isaiah 10:27. This power did the exact same thing that Isaiah said the anointing would do, and that is, *destroy yokes*!

What is the anointing that God promises will destroy yokes? According to the stories of the multitude (Luke 6:17-19), the woman with the issue of blood (Mark 5:25-34), and the man brought by four (Luke 5:17-26), the anointing is the virtue or, in other words, the healing power of God!

Therefore, if it is going to take the healing power of God for us to become free from the yoke of sickness, then it is time we begin to learn everything we possibly can about this power. We must come to know the laws that govern it, how it is obtained, and how to cooperate with it once it is administered to our bodies. We must not allow ourselves to remain ignorant of the very thing that will destroy the yoke of sickness off of us.

# 3 chapter

## Understanding
## The Healing
## Power of God

Volumes of books have been written about faith and the role it must be allowed to play in our lives, not only to obtain healing, but also to live and walk by faith. As knowledge has increased, our confidence in and cooperation with faith has increased and has been strengthened. Similarly, this book is dedicated to bringing an understanding of the healing power of God. The more we understand this power, the better equipped we are to have confidence in it and to cooperate with it.

For a moment, I am going to liken the healing power of God to something that is very common today: *electricity*. When it comes to electricity, in order to have confidence in it and cooperate with it, we must understand the laws that govern it. The more knowledge we have of these laws, the more we are capable of benefiting from electricity and being blessed by it.

Before the laws of electricity were discovered, electricity was *present*, but it was not much of a blessing to anyone. Electricity has been around since the creation of the world. It was present in Abraham's time, Moses' time, and even in Peter's time. But none of these men enjoyed the benefits of electricity. Yet I am sure that at times these men must have had situations arise where electricity would have made life much easier for them.

Even though these men and the people of their time needed electricity, electricity did not manifest itself just because they needed it. Even though electricity has been around since the creation of the world, it was not until men like Benjamin Franklin, Thomas Edison, and many others began to learn about the laws that governed it that man finally began to benefit from electricity. These men made it possible to benefit from and enjoy something that had been present since creation yet lay inactive. Once those laws were discovered and cooperated with, our life as we know it has not been the same.

## Like Electricity, the Healing Power Operates by Certain Laws

If all of the above is true concerning electricity, it is also true concerning God's healing power. This *power* to free us from the oppression of sickness and disease was supplied to us through the death, burial, and resurrection of our Lord and Savior, Jesus Christ. That event not only supplied the power to be saved from sin, but it also made available to mankind the power to be healed. The healing power has been present ever since that wonderful event occurred. And since that time, thousands have had the need to benefit from this power.

However, like electricity, there are laws that govern the operation of the healing power of God. The discovery of these laws makes it possible for us to cooperate with the power and be blessed by it. The laws that govern the operation of this power are not hidden from us. But if these laws are going to be discovered, we must go to the right location and begin to dig. The laws that govern this power can only be found in the Word of God. They are revealed to us through the ministry of Jesus, primarily through His words and His actions.

*There are many today who are concluding that the reason we do not see more people healed is because of a lack of power. So they have begun to pray for more power.*

Listening to what Jesus said and watching what Jesus did will reveal many things that will help us come to know and understand the laws that govern the healing power of God.

There are many today who are concluding that the reason we do not see more people healed is because of a lack of power. So they have begun to pray for more power. But we must accept the fact that through His death, burial, and resurrection, Jesus supplied all the healing power that we need! Praying for more healing power is as unnecessary today as praying for more *saving* power.

I am not praying that God will give us more power to save people with. Rather, I am teaching and encouraging sinners to believe and receive the saving power that was supplied to them through the sacrifice of Jesus on the Cross. I am doing the same thing with Christians who are oppressed by sickness. I am teaching and encouraging them to receive the healing power that Jesus supplied to them through His sacrifice on the Cross.

We do not have a power problem today. What we have is a *knowledge* problem. We are ignorant concerning the laws that govern the healing power of God. Therefore, we are incapable of obtaining it and cooperating with it in order to receive the healing that we so desperately need.

As I unveil in the following chapters the laws that govern the operation of God's healing power, I ask you to please read all of them carefully. Beginning to read them and not finishing them will cause you to come to wrong or incomplete conclusions. My desire is to bring into your life the things that the Lord has been so gracious to reveal to me through His wonderful Word. My prayer for you is that the eyes of your understanding be opened and that you may come to know the laws that govern the operation of the healing power of God! Once the laws are understood, you can connect or unite *your* faith with *His* power and keep your faith "connected" until any yoke of sickness in your life is destroyed!

4 chapter

# Law Number One:
## Just Because the Healing Power of God Is Present Does Not Guarantee You Will Be Healed

**LUKE 5:17-26**

17 And it came to pass on a certain day, as he was teaching, that there were Pharisees and doctors of the law sitting by, which were come out of every town of Galilee, and Judaea, and Jerusalem: and the power of the Lord was present to heal them.

18 And, behold, men brought in a bed a man which was taken with a palsy: and they sought means to bring him in, and to lay him before him.

19 And when they could not find by what way they might bring him in because of the multitude [the multitude of Pharisees and doctors of the Law], they went upon the housetop, and let him down through the tiling with his couch into the midst before Jesus.

20 And when he saw their faith, he said unto him, Man, thy sins are forgiven thee.

21 And the scribes and the Pharisees began to reason, saying, Who is this which speaketh blasphemies? Who can forgive sins, but God alone?

22 But when Jesus perceived their thoughts, he answering said unto them, What reason ye in your hearts?

23 Whether is easier, to say, Thy sins be forgiven thee; or to say, Rise up and walk?

24 But that ye may know that the Son of man hath power upon earth to forgive sins, (he said unto the sick of the palsy,) I say unto thee, Arise, and take up thy couch, and go into thine house.

25 And immediately he rose up before them, and took up that whereon he lay, and departed to his own house, glorifying God.

26 And they were all amazed, and they glorified God, and were filled with fear, saying, We have seen strange things to day.

In this passage of Scripture, we find Jesus teaching a room full of Pharisees and doctors of the Law. Verse 17 tells us that while He is teaching, *". . .the power of the Lord was present to heal them."*

The word "them" leads us to believe that there were many in this room who were in need of healing. It also implies that the power was present to heal *all* of "them" who were sick and not just certain ones. Since the power was present to heal them, God must have wanted them healed! God must have wanted every yoke of sickness destroyed that was in that room!

While Jesus is teaching, we are told of a man with palsy who was brought by four. They were endeavoring to get into the room where Jesus was. Trying every possible window and door, they found the crowd too large, and they were not allowed into the room. They were so convinced that help for their sick friend was inside that room that they went up on the housetop and tore a hole in the roof! Opening a hole large enough, they lowered the man with palsy into the midst before Jesus. As the story reveals, this man was gloriously healed with all those present as everlasting witnesses.

As Luke tells this wonderful story, you can almost imagine the expressions on the people's faces as they watched this man being lowered through this roof. They continued to be amazed when Jesus, instead of telling His disciples to go up on the roof and stop them from ripping it open, allowed them to continue.

When they finally lowered the sick man into the room, Jesus tells the man to "*. . .Arise, and take up thy couch, and go into thine house*" (Luke 5:24). This healed man leaves the house, and these astonished onlookers begin to say to one another, "Wow, we have seen strange things today!"(v. 26). We must come to the conclusion that this man's healing was talked about for a long time after it occurred. So many questions must have crossed the people's minds as they told the story over and over to those who were not present when it happened.

It is very evident that there were other sick people in this room before the man who was healed ever came on the scene. I am sure that these sick people must have gone back to their own homes, asking themselves one question: *Wait a minute! I had a sickness in my body; why wasn't I healed too? I just don't understand!*

I admit I have had the same question: "If the power of the Lord was present to heal *them*, then why was this man with the palsy the only person healed?" Luke tells us of no other person who was healed except for this man with the palsy who was brought by four. Yet Luke informs us that the power of the Lord was present to heal *them*. So it is very evident that the power was not only present to heal, but it was present to heal *them* before "*him*" ever came on the scene! This leads me to my first conclusion about the healing power of God: *Just because the power of the Lord is present to heal does not guarantee you will be healed.*

## The Woman With the Issue of Blood 'Stood Out' in the Crowd

In the Gospel of Mark, we find another example where the power of the Lord was present to heal *all*, and yet only one person received healing. It's time we understand that just because the healing power is present does not guarantee that we are going to be healed.

### MARK 5:22-34

22 And, behold, there cometh one of the rulers of the synagogue, Jairus by name; and when he saw him [Jesus], he fell at his feet,

23 And besought him greatly, saying, My little daughter lieth at the point of death: I pray thee, come and lay thy hands on her, that she may be healed; and she shall live.

24 And Jesus went with him; and much people followed him, and thronged him.

25 And a certain woman, which had an issue of blood twelve years,

26 And had suffered many things of many physicians, and
had spent all that she had, and was nothing bettered,
but rather grew worse,

27 When she had heard of Jesus, came in the press behind,
and touched his garment.

28 For she said, If I may touch but his clothes, I shall be
whole.

29 And straightway the fountain of her blood was dried
up; and she felt in her body that she was healed of that
plague.

30 And Jesus, immediately knowing in himself that virtue
had gone out of him, turned him about in the press, and
said, Who touched my clothes?

31 And his disciples said unto him, Thou seest the multitude thronging thee, and sayest thou, Who touched me?

32 And he looked round about to see her that had done
this thing.

33 But the woman fearing and trembling, knowing what
was done in her, came and fell down before him, and
told him all the truth.

34 And he said unto her, Daughter, thy faith hath made thee
whole; go in peace, and be whole of thy plague.

In verses 22 through 24, we find a man approaching Jesus
on behalf of his sick daughter. His name was Jairus. He requested
that Jesus come and lay His hands upon his daughter that she be
healed.

As Jesus is making His way to Jairus' house, Mark tells us
that a multitude is following Him. In fact, Mark gives us a vivid

description of this multitude. Verse 24 says, *"...MUCH PEOPLE followed him, and THRONGED him."* A further description of this crowd is given to us in verse 27: *"...[the woman with the issue of blood] came IN THE PRESS behind...."* And again, in verse 31: *"...Thou seest the MULTITUDE thronging thee...."*

Throughout the Gospels, we find account after account of crowds and multitudes that followed Jesus, and they always had among them people who were sick. This multitude in Mark chapter 5 that is following Jesus and Jairus must have been no exception. But it appears as we read this portion of Scripture that only one person in this crowd received healing, and that was the woman with the issue of blood.

Now the first question that must be asked is this: "Was the power of the Lord present to heal?" Yes! Verse 30 says, *"And Jesus, immediately knowing in himself that VIRTUE had gone out of him...."* What was this virtue? The word "virtue" used here means *power*. What kind of power went out of Him? It must have been *healing* power due to the fact that she was *healed*! It is very clear that the healing power was present.

Was this power present to heal all who were present or just the woman? It must have been present to heal all based on what Jesus said in verse 30: *"And Jesus, immediately knowing in himself that virtue had gone out of him, turned him about in the press, and said, Who touched my clothes?"* Notice Jesus did not turn around and say, "Now I was just touched, and virtue went out of Me. And I know it went into a woman who has had an issue of blood for twelve years. I knew you were coming, and that virtue was only for you."

No! The very fact that Jesus turned around and said, "*Who touched my clothes?*" tells me that the power was present to heal *all*. Glory! It was not just for the woman. But how many were healed in this crowd? One! Were there others who needed physical healing? Yes, I am sure there were! Then we must come to the conclusion once again that just because the power of the Lord is present to heal does not guarantee that every sick person is going to be healed.

## The Healing Power and the Residents of Jesus' Hometown

In Mark chapter 6, we find a third example that reveals to us that just because the power is present to heal does not guarantee that all the sick are going to be healed.

### MARK 6:1-6

1  And he went out from thence, and came into his own country; and his disciples follow him.

2  And when the sabbath day was come, he began to teach in the synagogue: and many hearing him were astonished, saying, From whence hath this man these things? and what wisdom is this which is given unto him, that even such mighty works are wrought by his hands?

3  Is not this the carpenter, the son of Mary, the brother of James, and Joses, and of Juda, and Simon? and are not his sisters here with us? And they were offended at him.

4  But Jesus said unto them, A prophet is not without honour, but in his own country, and among his own kin, and in his own house.

5    And he could there do no mighty work, save that he laid his hands upon a few sick folk, and healed them.

6    And he marvelled because of their unbelief. And he went round about the villages, teaching.


Jesus is in His hometown ministering. Verse 5 gives us a summary of His success: *"And he could there do no mighty work, save that he laid his hands upon a few sick folk, and healed them."*

Notice it did not say, "And He *would* there do no mighty work." It said, "And He *could* there do no mighty work." Verse 6 tells us *why* Jesus could there do no mighty work: *"And he marvelled because of their UNBELIEF. . . ."* It did not say, "And He marveled because of the lack of power." It said He marveled at their unbelief. *It was their unbelief that caused them not to benefit from the power that was present to heal.*

This account reveals that there were a few who did receive healing. But due to Jesus' reaction in verse 6, I am very comfortable in coming to the conclusion that the power of the Lord was present to heal more than just the few who did get healed.

Mark 6:6 says. *"And he marvelled because of their unbelief. And he went round about the villages, teaching."* Jesus' marveling informs me that He knew that the power was present to set every sick person free in His hometown. Although the power isn't

*Need does not cause the healing power to manifest itself and heal you.*

mentioned specifically, it is very apparent that the power was present to heal more than those who were healed. There was no power shortage there while Jesus was ministering. If the other sick people had not been in unbelief, they could have received their healing also. Their yoke could have been destroyed too. Through this experience of Jesus in His hometown, we come to understand that just because the healing power is present does not mean that all the sick are automatically going to be set free.

The accounts given to us in Luke 5, Mark 5, and Mark 6 reveal to us that just because the power of the Lord is present does not automatically guarantee that you are going to be healed. They also reveal to us that your need for healing does not cause God's healing power to manifest itself and heal you. There were people in each of these stories who needed to be healed, yet they remained bound by their yokes.

I will never forget a little lady who came to one of my services and said to me with tears, "I know I will be healed."

I responded, "How do you know, Sister?" She said, "Because I need to see my grandchild graduate from high school." I thought to myself, *Need does not cause the healing power to manifest itself and heal you.*

Remember the example of electricity that I used. As I said, I am sure that many in Moses' time must have *needed* electricity, but electricity did not manifest itself just because they needed it. Let's face it, the world needs to become saved, but just because they need to be saved does not make the saving power of God manifest and just save them on its own.

Another lady once said to me, "Glory! I know I will be healed because I have the greatest need in this room to be healed." She had previously evaluated the others in the service and had come to the conclusion that her problem was the most severe! But it is not how desperate you are or how sick you are that determines whether you will receive or not. What matters is, have you connected *your* faith to *His* power?

The first thing we must understand concerning the healing power of God is, *just because the power of the Lord is present to heal does not automatically guarantee that you will be healed*. Since this is true, let us continue to learn about all the laws that govern the operation of the healing power of God so that we may profit personally from the healing power instead of just continuing to observe *others* benefiting from the anointing that destroys the yoke!

# Law Number Two:
## The Power of the Lord Can Be Present To Heal and Your Senses Be Totally Unaware of It

In the previous chapter, we learned that just because the healing power is present does not guarantee you will be healed.

The second law that we must come to understand about the healing power of God is this: *The healing power can be present to heal and there be no physical evidence of its presence whatsoever*. In other words, it can be present and you not *feel* its presence.

People come to me and say, "There is no healing power in our church." My response is always, "How do you know there is no power?" They reply, "Because no one is getting healed. We haven't seen anyone healed in our church in months."

What these people are saying is that the only way you can tell whether or not the power is present is by *seeing* people get healed, and if people are not being healed, then the power is not present. But if this be true, then we must also conclude that if people are not being saved — born again — then the power to save is not present. Yet I have attended many services where I knew that there were unbelievers or sinners present. The pastor preached a salvation message, but when the altar call was given, no one raised his hand in response, no one moved, and the service was dismissed with no one born again.

Was the power to save present? Absolutely! Yet there was no physical evidence given to the sinner that the saving power of God was present. If you went by what you saw, you could have concluded that the power to save was not present. However, the power *was* present to save.

We must not go by outward manifestations to determine whether the power is present or not present. The power of the Lord can be present and yet there be no physical manifestation of it whatsoever.

The following passage of Scripture illustrates this point.

### LUKE 5:17-26

17 And it came to pass on a certain day, as he was teaching, that there were Pharisees and doctors of the law sitting by, which were come out of every town of Galilee, and Judaea, and Jerusalem: and the power of the Lord was present to heal them.

18 And, behold, men brought in a bed a man which was taken with a palsy: and they sought means to bring him in, and to lay him before him.

19 And when they could not find by what way they might bring him in because of the multitude, they went upon

the housetop, and let him down through the tiling with his couch into the midst before Jesus.

20 And when he saw their faith, he said unto him, Man, thy sins are forgiven thee.

21 And the scribes and the Pharisees began to reason, saying, Who is this which speaketh blasphemies? Who can forgive sins, but God alone?

22 But when Jesus perceived their thoughts, he answering said unto them, What reason ye in your hearts?

23 Whether is easier, to say, Thy sins be forgiven thee; or to say, Rise up and walk?

24 But that ye may know that the Son of man hath power upon earth to forgive sins, (he said unto the sick of the palsy,) I say unto thee, Arise, and take up thy couch, and go into thine house.

25 And immediately he rose up before them, and took up that whereon he lay, and departed to his own house, glorifying God.

26 And they were all amazed, and they glorified God, and were filled with fear, saying, We have seen strange things to day.

Here again is the account of this man with the palsy being let down through the roof. Luke unquestionably reveals to us that the power of the Lord was present in this room to heal long before the man with the palsy came on the scene.

Verse 17 says, *"And it came to pass on a certain day, as he was teaching, that there were Pharisees and doctors of the law sitting by, which were come out of every town of Galilee, and*

*Judaea, and Jerusalem: and the power of the Lord was present to heal them."*

Verse 18 says, *"And, behold, men brought in a bed a man which was taken with a palsy: and they sought means to bring him in, and to lay him before him."*

It appears that before this man with the palsy was healed, the people in this room were totally unaware that the power of the Lord was present to heal them. No one was being healed; there were no outward manifestations of the power's presence. Yet even though they could not feel it or see it, that power was present. If it had not been for the man with the palsy being healed, no one in that crowd would have ever known that the power was present to heal.

Too many people are determining whether or not the power to heal is present through what they can see or feel. This happens often. For example, a minister might come to a church to hold special services. The people in the church have never seen or heard him minister before. In the first service, he preaches a message on healing and asks if people would like to have hands laid on them for healing.

*Your senses are an unsafe guide when it comes to determining whether or not the healing power is present.*

Four brave souls come forward. The minister lays his hands on the first person, and that person "falls out" under the power and almost gets knocked back into the row of chairs behind him. The second person falls under the power; the third likewise falls under the power. And by the time he gets to the fourth person, the altar is full of people waiting on all sides to get in line! Why? Because they came to the conclusion by watching people fall under the power of God that the power of the Lord was present to heal. As a result, they became convinced, *based on what they saw*, that the healing power was present!

These people would not believe the power was present at the first invitation. But the moment two or three people were "knocked down" under the power of God, the altar was full of people. Can you see that they were using their senses to determine whether or not the healing power was present?

Many people are guided by their senses. But it is very evident from Luke 5:17-26 that the power of the Lord can be present and your senses be totally unaware of it. *Your senses are an unsafe guide when it comes to determining whether or not the healing power is present.*

Another example of the power of the Lord being present without any *evidence* of its presence is found in Luke 4. No evidence of the power's presence was given to the senses of those in attendance where Jesus read the Scriptures that said He was anointed to heal.

LUKE 4:16-30

16 And he came to Nazareth, where he had been brought up: and, as his custom was, he went into the synagogue on the sabbath day, and stood up for to read.

17 And there was delivered unto him the book of the prophet Esaias. And when he had opened the book, he found the place where it was written,

18 The Spirit of the Lord is upon me, because he hath anointed me to preach the gospel to the poor; he hath sent me to heal the brokenhearted, to preach deliverance

to the captives, and recovering of sight to the blind, to set at liberty them that are bruised,

19 To preach the acceptable year of the Lord.

20 And he closed the book, and he gave it again to the minister, and sat down. And the eyes of all them that were in the synagogue were fastened on him.

21 And he began to say unto them, This day is this scripture fulfilled in your ears.

22 And all bare him witness, and wondered at the gracious words which proceeded out of his mouth. And they said, Is not this Joseph's son?

23 And he said unto them, Ye will surely say unto me this proverb, Physician, heal thyself: whatsoever we have heard done in Capernaum, do also here in thy country.

24 And he said, Verily I say unto you, No prophet is accepted in his own country.

25 But I tell you of a truth, many widows were in Israel in the days of Elias, when the heaven was shut up three years and six months, when great famine was throughout all the land;

26 But unto none of them was Elias sent, save unto Sarepta, a city of Sidon, unto a woman that was a widow.

27 And many lepers were in Israel in the time of Eliseus the prophet; and none of them was cleansed, saving Naaman the Syrian.

28 And all they in the synagogue, when they heard these things, were filled with wrath,

29 And rose up, and thrust him out of the city, and led him unto the brow of the hill whereon their city was built, that they might cast him down headlong.

30 But he passing through the midst of them went his way.

When Jesus said, "*. . .This day is this scripture fulfilled in your ears*" (v. 21), He was actually saying, "The power to heal you is present now; the power to deliver you is present now; the power to liberate you is here *now*"! Yet Jesus did not give the people one single miracle to help them believe that the healing power was present. He simply stood in their midst and proclaimed to them that the power to heal was present and available to them right then. He asked them to believe that the power was present based on His Word and His Word alone.

As I read this portion of Scripture one day, the Lord said to me, "I want you to notice that when I said, 'This day is this scripture fulfilled in your ears,' I was asking them to believe that the power was present to heal them based solely on my words without giving them any physical evidence of its presence whatsoever."

Those people in Luke 4 did not believe that the power was present. They responded by saying, "Wait a minute; we grew up with Him. His dad did some carpentry work for us. He doesn't possess any special power. How can He free us? How can He heal us? His brothers and sisters are here with us; we know this guy!"

You see, they went by what they *knew* and *saw* to determine whether the power was present to heal or not. They came to the conclusion so strongly that the power was *not* present that they "*. . .rose up, and thrust him out of the city, and led* *him unto the brow of the hill whereon their city was built, that they might cast him down headlong"* (v. 29).

Their senses were an unsafe guide in determining whether or not the power was present. It was impossible for them to go by what they saw or felt to determine whether or not the power was present. Jesus was requiring them to *believe* that the power was present without the aid of a miracle to *prove* that the power was present. Therefore, we as Christians must not look to what we feel or see to determine whether or not the power is present. If we should lean toward these two areas of feeling and seeing, we will be sorely disappointed.

*Your senses are an unsafe guide when it comes to determining whether or not the healing power is present!*

So many today associate the healing power with certain people or ministers. For example, I have noticed that some people try to determine whether or not the power is present by calling the church to ask who the speaker is going to be on a particular night. In other words, if minister So-and-so is not going to be ministering, then they see no need to attend, because they believe that the power will not be present if So-and-so is not ministering. I find this type of thinking so sad.

The healing power of God does not just show up when certain ministers are speaking! The healing power does not manifest itself only in certain types of services. No, we must understand this second law concerning the healing power of God: *The power of the Lord can be present to heal and your senses be totally unaware of it.*

chapter

# Law Number Three:
## In Order To Benefit From the Healing Power, You Must First *Believe* That the Power Is Present

LUKE 4:16-30

16 And he came to Nazareth, where he had been brought up: and, as his custom was, he went into the synagogue on the sabbath day, and stood up for to read.

17 And there was delivered unto him the book of the prophet Esaias. And when he had opened the book, he found the place where it was written,

18 The Spirit of the Lord is upon me, because he hath anointed me to preach the gospel to the poor; he hath sent me to heal the brokenhearted, to preach deliverance to the captives, and recovering of sight to the blind, to set at liberty them that are bruised,

19 To preach the acceptable year of the Lord.

20 And he closed the book, and he gave it again to the minister, and sat down. And the eyes of all them that were in the synagogue were fastened on him.

21 And he began to say unto them, This day is this scripture fulfilled in your ears.

22 And all bare him witness, and wondered at the gracious words which proceeded out of his mouth. And they said, Is not this Joseph's son?

23 And he said unto them, Ye will surely say unto me this proverb, Physician, heal thyself: whatsoever we have heard done in Capernaum, do also here in thy country.

24 And he said, Verily I say unto you, No prophet is accepted in his own country.

25 But I tell you of a truth, many widows were in Israel in the days of Elias, when the heaven was shut up three years and six months, when great famine was throughout all the land;

26 But unto none of them was Elias sent, save unto Sarepta, a city of Sidon, unto a woman that was a widow.

27 And many lepers were in Israel in the time of Eliseus the prophet; and none of them was cleansed, saving Naaman the Syrian.

28 And all they in the synagogue, when they heard these things, were filled with wrath,

29 And rose up, and thrust him out of the city, and led him unto the brow of the hill whereon their city was built, that they might cast him down headlong.

30 But he passing through the midst of them went his way.

In verse 21, Jesus declared that the Scripture He read was fulfilled "this day." He was boldly proclaiming that the power of the Lord was present to heal, liberate, or set them free. But one question comes to mind: Did the people who were present *believe* that the power was present? No! This attitude is revealed through their response in verse 22: *"And all bare him witness, and wondered at the gracious words which proceeded out of his mouth. And they said, Is not this Joseph's son?"*

*We must understand this law which reveals to us that if we are going to benefit from the healing power of God, we must believe that it is present now to heal!*

As I said previously, their response was, "Wait a minute. You're Joseph's son. We grew up with you! You don't have any special power to set us free. Who are you trying to kid?"

Jesus responded to their disbelief by saying, ". . .*Verily I say unto you, No prophet is accepted in his own country"* (v. 24). Their unbelief is also revealed in verses 28 and 29: *"And all they in the synagogue, when they heard these things, were filled with wrath, And rose up, and thrust him out of the city, and led him unto the brow of the hill whereon their city was built, that they might cast him down headlong."*

They did not believe that the healing power was present, thereby making it impossible for them to benefit from it. No one was healed in this crowd, and it was the result of their unbelief. But in spite of their unbelief, the power to heal was very much present. We must understand this law which reveals to us that if we are going to benefit from the healing power of God, we must *believe* that it is present *now* to heal!

The examples that follow are of people who believed that the power of the Lord was present to heal, and we will see that they benefited from that power as a result. As we read the following accounts, notice it did not require the faith of the individual to cause the power to become *present*. But it *did* require the faith of the individual to *benefit* from the power that was present.

In every case listed, the recipient believed that the power was present to heal, making it possible for him or her to benefit from it.

## The Woman With the Issue of Blood

MARK 5:25-34

25  And a certain woman, which had an issue of blood twelve years,

26  And had suffered many things of many physicians, and had spent all that she had, and was nothing bettered, but rather grew worse,

27  When she had heard of Jesus, came in the press behind, and touched his garment.

28  For she said, If I may touch but his clothes, I shall be whole.

29  And straightway the fountain of her blood was dried up; and she felt in her body that she was healed of that plague.

30  And Jesus, immediately knowing in himself that virtue had gone out of him, turned him about in the press, and said, Who touched my clothes?

31 And his disciples said unto him, Thou seest the multitude thronging thee, and sayest thou, Who touched me?

32 And he looked round about to see her that had done this thing.

33 But the woman fearing and trembling, knowing what was done in her, came and fell down before him, and told him all the truth.

34 And he said unto her, Daughter, thy faith hath made thee whole; go in peace, and be whole of thy plague.

This woman with the issue of blood had been very ill for twelve years. Spending all that she had and suffering many things of many physicians, she had come to the end of her ability to change her circumstance. She was getting worse day by day.

Then someone came to her and told her about Jesus. She immediately set out to find Him and to "touch but His clothes," being confident that she would be healed. Her confidence and determination were fueled by one thing: She *believed* that Jesus had the power that she needed to destroy the yoke of sickness off of her.

Let me ask you a question: As this woman is pressing toward the hem of Jesus' garment, does she believe that the power is present to heal her? *Emphatically, yes!* Did she benefit from the power? *Absolutely!*

*If we are going to obtain healing as this woman did, we must believe the same things she believed.* If *she* believed that the power was present, then *we* must believe that the power is present.

Remember, if you are going to benefit from the healing power of God, you must first believe that it is present.

## The Man Who Was Let Down Through the Roof

### LUKE 5:17-26

17 And it came to pass on a certain day, as he was teaching, that there were Pharisees and doctors of the law sitting by, which were come out of every town of Galilee, and Judaea, and Jerusalem: and the power of the Lord was present to heal them.

18 And, behold, men brought in a bed a man which was taken with a palsy: and they sought means to bring him in, and to lay him before him.

19 And when they could not find by what way they might bring him in because of the multitude, they went upon the housetop, and let him down through the tiling with his couch into the midst before Jesus.

20 And when he saw their faith, he said unto him, Man, thy sins are forgiven thee.

21 And the scribes and the Pharisees began to reason, saying, Who is this which speaketh blasphemies? Who can forgive sins, but God alone?

22 But when Jesus perceived their thoughts, he answering said unto them, What reason ye in your hearts?

23 Whether is easier, to say, Thy sins be forgiven thee; or to say, Rise up and walk?

24 But that ye may know that the Son of man hath power upon earth to forgive sins, (he said unto the sick of the

palsy,) I say unto thee, Arise, and take up thy couch, and go into thine house.

25 And immediately he rose up before them, and took up that whereon he lay, and departed to his own house, glorifying God.

26 And they were all amazed, and they glorified God, and were filled with fear, saying, We have seen strange things to day.

Once again we read of the man who was "brought by four" and let down from the roof into the midst before Jesus. I think it is very clear that this man and his friends believed that the power was present, thus making it possible for them to benefit from the power. If they had *not* believed that the power was present, the man's condition would have remained as it was. Their belief that the power was present kept them going in spite of the obstacles they encountered.

Unbelief will cause your situation to remain as it is. Unbelief will keep you a prisoner to sickness. You must believe that the healing power is present if you are going to benefit from it.

### The Centurion's Servant Who Was on His Deathbed

LUKE 7:2-10

2 And a certain centurion's servant, who was dear unto him, was sick, and ready to die.

3 And when he heard of Jesus, he sent unto him the elders of the Jews, beseeching him that he would come and heal his servant.

4 And when they came to Jesus, they besought him instantly, saying, That he was worthy for whom he should do this:

5 For he loveth our nation, and he hath built us a synagogue.

6 Then Jesus went with them. And when he was now not far from the house, the centurion sent friends to him, saying unto him, Lord, trouble not thyself: for I am not worthy that thou shouldest enter under my roof:

7 Wherefore neither thought I myself worthy to come unto thee: but say in a word, and my servant shall be healed.

8 For I also am a man set under authority, having under me soldiers, and I say unto one, Go, and he goeth; and to another, Come, and he cometh; and to my servant, Do this, and he doeth it.

9 When Jesus heard these things, he marvelled at him, and turned him about, and said unto the people that followed him, I say unto you, I have not found so great faith, no, not in Israel.

10 And they that were sent, returning to the house, found the servant whole that had been sick.

Here is another example of a person who benefited from the power that was present. It all began when the centurion obtained and acted on the belief that the healing power was present. (The starting point on the road to healing must be the belief that the healing power is present. Without this belief, things will remain as they are.)

How did the centurion obtain this belief that the healing power was present? He obtained it through *knowledge*. Notice verse 3: *"And when he HEARD of Jesus, he sent unto him the elders of the Jews, beseeching him that he would come and heal his servant."*

Someone told this centurion about Jesus and the power to heal. As the centurion heard, he accepted it as truth and sent the elders of the Jews to beseech Jesus to come and heal his servant. As Jesus approached the centurion's home, the centurion saw Him coming and sent out another group of friends to give Jesus a message. The message was, *". . .Lord, trouble not thyself: for I am not worthy that thou shouldest enter under my roof: Wherefore neither thought I myself worthy to come unto thee: BUT SAY IN A WORD, and my servant shall be healed"* (Luke 7:6,7).

This message was sent by a man who believed that the healing power was present to heal!

The healing examples given to us in the Gospels have been given to us to learn what these men and women did in order to obtain their healing. We must follow their examples, not so much the specifics of what they *did*, but, rather, the specifics of what they *believed*.

Ask yourself as you read the different healing examples in the Gospels: What did the people who were healed believe? What did the people who were *not* healed believe? Answering these questions will shed much light on why some people are healed today and why some are not. Those in the Gospels who were healed have much in common with one another. Their examples have enough in common that as you read them, you will see a pattern develop.

(However, you must understand that there are two types of healing examples given to us in the Gospels. The first type of examples are of those who *came to Jesus* to be healed. These were the people to whom Jesus would turn and say, "Your faith hath made you whole!" *These were the people who initiated the healing process with their faith.* In other words, they did not wait for Jesus to come to them; *they* came to *Jesus*.

> *In order to benefit from the healing power of God, the recipient must believe that the healing power is present!*

The second type of examples are of those whom *Jesus approached*. These are the people to whom Jesus was led by the Holy Ghost, and they received healing as the result of manifestations of the Holy Ghost. *These people did not initiate the healing process; rather, the Holy Ghost initiated it through Jesus.*

However, in this chapter we are focusing our attention on some of those who came to Jesus to be healed; *they* approached *Him*. Look at this group very carefully. Discover and understand what they believed and allow them to be a model that you can follow right into healing!)

### The Woman Who Came to Jesus on Behalf of Her Daughter

MATTHEW 15:21-28

21 Then Jesus went thence, and departed into the coasts of Tyre and Sidon.

22 And, behold, a woman of Canaan came out of the same coasts, and cried unto him, saying, Have mercy on me, O Lord, thou Son of David; my daughter is grievously vexed with a devil.

23 But he answered her not a word. And his disciples came and besought him, saying, Send her away; for she crieth after us.

24 But he answered and said, I am not sent but unto the lost sheep of the house of Israel.

25 Then came she and worshipped him, saying, Lord, help me.

26 But he answered and said, It is not meet to take the children's bread, and to cast it to dogs.

27 And she said, Truth, Lord: yet the dogs eat of the crumbs which fall from their masters' table.

28 Then Jesus answered and said unto her, O woman, great is thy faith: be it unto thee even as thou wilt. And her daughter was made whole from that very hour.

This woman's determination reveals to me that she believed that the power of the Lord was present to heal. She was so persuaded of this fact that she was not going to leave the presence of Jesus without it! She believed that the power of the Lord was present, and she obviously benefited from it!

Throughout this chapter, we have seen examples of people who did not believe that the power was present, and we have seen examples of those who *did* believe that the power was present. It is very evident that we must believe that the power of the Lord is present in order to benefit from it. Failure to do so will cause us to remain bound by sickness and disease.

*In order to benefit from the healing power of God, the recipient must believe that the healing power is present!*

# 7 chapter

# Law Number Four:
There Are Two
Ways the Power of
the Lord Is Made
Present To Heal

If we must believe that the healing power is present in order to benefit from it, then we must understand *how* the power becomes present to heal. Now I am sure you understand that the death, burial, and resurrection of Jesus was the method by which our Heavenly Father made salvation and healing available to mankind. Since that wonderful event, the healing power has been available to any believer who becomes aware of it and receives it into his or her life.

In order for the power to be obtained, it must first become present to those who need to be healed. Since Jesus is no longer walking the streets of Israel — since He is no longer on the earth physically — how can we who have need of healing come in contact with the healing power of God? There are two vehicles by which the healing power of God is made present to heal us today.

## The Word of God Is the First Vehicle by Which the Healing Power Comes

*The first and primary way the power to heal is made present to us is through the Word!* When we read scriptures that promise us healing, the power to heal is made available to us. When we hear someone preach or teach from the Bible that God has supplied healing for us through Jesus Christ, the power to heal is at that moment made present. *The power always accompanies the Word.*

So many have said to me, "There's no power to heal in our church; no one is being healed in our church." What they are really saying is, "I'm not going to believe that the power is present until I see someone healed. If no one is being healed, then that must mean there is no power present." The only way I can respond to this kind of thinking is to ask them one question: "Is your minister preaching or teaching the fact that Jesus supplied healing to us through His crucifixion?"

"Oh, yes," they respond. "He teaches on healing all the time."

Well, if that pastor is teaching on healing, then the power to heal is present and available! When the Word comes, *power* comes!

Let me illustrate this point. In Matthew 14:22-33, we find that Jesus had sent the disciples ahead of Him in a boat to go "to the other side" (v. 22). Later, Jesus, needing to go to the other side but finding Himself without a boat, began to cross the lake by walking on top of the water!

As Jesus approached the boat, the disciples mistook Him for a spirit. Jesus immediately calmed them by informing them, "It is I" (v. 27). The moment Peter recognized Him, he requested permission to also walk on the water. Jesus spoke one word to Peter; He said, "Come" (v. 29).

*Our obedience releases the power within the Word. Where there is no obedience, the power remains unreleased.*

The moment Jesus spoke that one word, power to walk on water was made available to Peter! Power to walk on water was delivered to Peter through the word "come." Before this word "come" was given to Peter, he did not have available to him the power to walk on water. Then the instant Peter acted on the word that was spoken, he unlocked the power that was within that little word and did something he had only dreamed of doing before!

If there is anything we as believers need to learn about the Word, it is that within every promise or command is the power for us to change the situations we encounter in this life. *Our obedience releases the power within the Word.* Where there is no obedience, the power remains unreleased.

You remember in the sixth chapter of Joshua that the children of Israel had entered the Promised Land. Suddenly, they come in contact with a massive city called Jericho. After Joshua sends two spies into the city, God instructs Joshua as to what the children of Israel must do in order to conquer this city. They are told by God to make a trip around the walls one time a day for six days. On the seventh day, they were to compass the city seven times, and at the end of the seventh trip, they were to shout, and the walls would come tumbling down!

Are you aware of the fact that when those instructions were given to Joshua, power to tumble a city's walls was made available to Israel? But if they had not obeyed the instructions, they would have remained powerless to tumble the walls; those walls would probably still be standing today.

But they obeyed God's instructions, releasing the power that accompanied the instructions, and the walls could not keep from falling!

Romans 10:9 says, *"That if thou shalt confess with thy mouth the Lord Jesus, and shalt believe in thine heart that God hath raised him from the dead, thou shalt be saved."* The moment this scripture is presented to a sinner, power to become saved is made available to him. *Obedience* to this verse releases the *power* within this verse. Do you understand there is enough power within this verse when released to deliver a sinner out of the kingdom of darkness and translate him into the Kingdom of God's dear Son (Col. 1:13)? *Glory!*

Romans 6:17 and 18 says, *"But God be thanked, that ye were the servants of sin, but ye have obeyed from the heart that form of doctrine which was delivered you. Being then made free from sin, ye became the servants of righteousness."*

These two verses show us clearly how we were made free from sin. They reveal to us that while we were sinners, someone delivered unto us the "form of doctrine" (remember, power accompanies the Word). We obeyed from the heart (remember, obedience releases the power within the Word). Then we were made free from sin.

What would have happened if we had never heard the Word concerning salvation? Then power to become free from sin would never have become available to us.

Failure to tell sinners about Jesus and about Romans 10:9 keeps them from the very power that they need in order to become saved. Do you understand that this is the very reason why Jesus in Mark 16:15 says, *". . .Go ye into all the world, and preach the gospel to every creature"*?

God is not withholding the power to become saved from the sinner; *we* are when we fail to tell the sinner what the Word says about salvation. When we tell others about Jesus, we are making power to be saved available to them. Then by obeying Romans 10:9, the sinner *releases* the power to be saved, and it makes him a new creature.

James knew what he was doing when he strongly encouraged each of us to be doers of the Word and not just hearers only (James 1:22). James must have known that obedience releases the power within the Word!

The Bible illustrates the Word as *seed.* Over and over again, the Bible uses the seed to teach us how the Word operates. In fact "the Word" and "seed" are synonymous terms in many places in the Bible. First Peter 1:23 is a clear example. It says, *"Being born again, not of corruptible seed, but of incorruptible, by the word of God, which liveth and abideth for ever."*

The parable of the sower is another excellent example of "the Word" and "seed" being used interchangeably. This story is found in Luke chapter 8. As Jesus explains the parable to His disciples, He plainly states in verse 11 that the seed is the Word of God. Jesus said, *"Now the parable is this: The seed is the word of God"* (Luke 8:11). By using the seed, Jesus is teaching us through this parable how the Word produces results, for we all know how the seed produces fruit.

When it comes to a natural seed, we understand that there is power within each seed to reproduce itself. If you have in your hand a few apple seeds, you are actually holding little containers of power. Plant them, water them, and you will release the power within those seeds. This released power is strong enough to push upward a fragile blade through two to five inches of soil and produce enough roots so that within two years, even a grown man would have difficulty pulling it out of the ground!

Remember, as Jesus uses the seed to illustrate the Word, He is actually teaching us the characteristics of His Word. He is taking something we are very familiar with — seed — to teach us about something we have difficulty understanding — the Word.

Now you understand that the power within a seed in the natural must be released through the method of *planting and watering*. The power within the Word must be released through the method of *obedience*. No planting and no watering mean no results from the seed. Likewise, no obedience means no results from the Word.

*If we really understood that God's Word is full of life and power, we would no longer treat it with such disrespect.*

Hebrews 4:12 says, *"For the word of God is quick, and powerful, and sharper than any twoedged sword, piercing even to the dividing asunder of soul and spirit, and of the joints and marrow, and is a discerner of the thoughts and intents of the heart."*

One translation says, "For the word of God is living and powerful." Another translations says, "For the word of God is full of life and power." And another says, "For whatever God says to us is full of living power."

Do we really grasp the significance of this truth? If we really understood that God's Word is full of life and power, we would no longer treat it with such disrespect. We would place a new and higher value on the Word. Questioning it would be a thing of the past. Hearing the Word and not doing it would be something we only *used* to do. The Word of God is full of power, but the power is only released through obedience.

As one translation of Hebrews 4:12 said, "For whatever God says to us is full of living power," we understand that power always accompanies the Word! For example, anytime we read or hear passages in the Word instructing us as to how we are to conduct ourselves as parents, power to raise behaved and happy children is delivered unto us. Obedience to those passages will release the power within them, and we will see our home life change as a result.

The moment we read or hear passages instructing husbands and wives as to how to conduct ourselves with each other, power to have a happy marriage is made available to us. Yet instead of releasing the power of those verses through obedience, we spend all of our time screaming at the devil, rebuking him, and commanding him to leave our home. Happy homes are not the result of screaming at the devil but, rather, of the power that is released through our obedience to the Word. If we will listen and obey, the truth will set us free!

I am still talking about one way that the healing power is made present or available to us: *by hearing or reading the Word concerning healing!* So if your pastor is teaching or preaching about healing, you can be confident that the power to heal is present in your church. If people are not being healed, instead of blaming it on the absence of power, you might need to change your thoughts to the absence of *obedience*. Obedience to the Word releases the power within the Word!

The power of God always accompanies the Word of God. As I said, we can read the Word or hear the Word concerning healing and automatically have the healing power present and available to us. And as illustrated in the ministry of Jesus, the healing power accompanies the Word of God when the Word on healing is taught.

In Luke 5:17 we see a very interesting revelation concerning the power accompanying the Word. Verse 17 says, *"And it came to pass on a certain day, as he* [Jesus] *was teaching, that there were Pharisees and doctors of the law sitting by, which were come out of every town of Galilee, and Judaea, and Jerusalem: and the power of the Lord was present to heal them."*

Notice Jesus was teaching, and Luke tells us that *". . .the power of the Lord was present to heal them."* The power accompanies the Word. What I find interesting in this passage is that the power of the Lord was present to heal, and Jesus wasn't even preaching! He wasn't screaming; He wasn't running around the room! He wasn't jumping over any pews! The Bible tells us that He was was simply *teaching*.

Too many have the idea that the power of the Lord is only present when they are experiencing a certain type of service. Some think that the power is only present when they are in a high-energy, preaching type of service. But Jesus reveals to us through this event in Luke 5 that the power can be present even in a teaching session! We must understand that power always accompanies the Word of God, *not* a particular type of service.

So the primary way that the power to heal is made present is through the Word. Whether you're hearing about healing taught in a church service or through a cassette or on TV, the *power* to heal is made present through the *Word*. You can even cause the power to become present to heal by reading healing scriptures in the privacy of your own home. Why? Because whenever the Word concerning healing is proclaimed or read about from the Word of God, power accompanies it every time.

The power — healing power — always accompanies the Word! Now remember in the previous chapter, I stated that in order for a person to benefit from the power that is present, he or she must *believe* it is present. Therefore, we need to ask ourselves, "Do we believe that the power to heal is present when the subject of healing is taught or read about from the Word of God? Or are we still waiting for our favorite minister to come to town before we will believe that the power is present? Do we *believe* that power accompanies the promises in the Word?"

### The Power Can Be Present Even if Unbelief Is Also Present

Before I mention the second method by which the healing power of the Lord becomes present, I would like to add one more thought. This additional thought comes from Luke 5:17-26. We must understand that it does not take everyone in the room to be in "one accord" to get the power present to heal.

Luke 5:17 says, *"And it came to pass on a certain day, as he was teaching, that there were Pharisees and doctors of the law sitting by, which were come out of every town of Galilee, and Judaea, and Jerusalem: and the power of the Lord was present to heal them.* " Notice *who* Jesus is teaching — Pharisees and doctors of the law (Scribes) — two sects of the Jewish religion. You realize that time after time, members of these two sects would question and challenge Jesus' doctrine and ministry. The Pharisees were not on Jesus' side at all. So what you have is a room full of unbelievers — skeptics — and Jesus is teaching them.

This room is so full of those who oppose Jesus that "the four" could not get their sick friend into the room. But the Bible says in Luke 5:17 that while Jesus was teaching, ". . .*the power of the Lord was present to heal them.* " This helps me understand that you do not have to have a room full of people in one accord in order to have the power of the Lord present. You do not have to have a room full of believers using their faith, believing that the power will become present, in order to get the power of the Lord present to heal. I don't know about you, but that is good news to me!

I was in New York teaching once and had some extra time off one afternoon. One of my former students offered to take me to New York City. Never having had the opportunity to visit this city, I agreed to go with him. In New York City, we stopped at a certain traffic light, and as I looked to my left, I saw a flatbed truck blocking one of the roads that met at that particular intersection. Standing on the flatbed truck was a man preaching the Gospel of salvation to those who were standing nearby. As I observed the crowd that had gathered, it looked as though many were making fun of the preacher. Others ignored him and continued on their way. It did not appear as if there were a lot of other believers helping him. It was very apparent that skeptics were the majority.

As our light turned green, we began moving again, and I thought to myself, *That man was preaching the Gospel of salvation to those people; and even though it appears as if no one was present but skeptics, I am convinced that the power of the Lord was present to save those people!*

*All it takes to get the healing power to become present is someone to teach or preach about healing. The power to heal follows the Gospel of healing. Power accompanies the Word!*

It did not take all those people in that crowd to be in agreement — using their faith and believing that the power to save would become present — in order to get the power present to save! No, and we know that we could be ministering to a room full of unbelievers, preaching the Gospel of salvation to them, and yet the power of the Lord would be present to save them all. Why? Because the power to save is made present when the Gospel of salvation is preached or taught.

Likewise, we must understand that it does not take everyone in a church or a service to be in one accord — using their faith, believing for the power of the Lord to become present — in order to get the power present to heal. All it takes to get the healing power to become present is someone to teach or preach about healing. The power to heal follows the *Gospel of healing.* Power accompanies the Word!

However, although it does not take everyone in a church or a service using his faith to cause the power to become present, it *will* take faith on the part of the recipient to *benefit* from the power that is made present as the result of the teaching or preaching of the Word.

For example, it does not take the faith of the sinner to make the power of the Lord to save to become present. But it *does* take faith on the part of the sinner to *receive* the saving power into his or her life. Ephesians 2:8 says, *"For by grace are ye saved through faith; and that not of yourselves: it is the gift of God."*

Similarly, it does not take the faith of the sick to cause the power to heal to become present. But it will take faith on the part of the sick to receive and benefit from the healing power that was made present through the teaching or preaching of the Word.

### Manifestations of the Gifts of the Holy Spirit Are the Second Vehicle by Which the Power Comes

There is another method by which the healing power can be made present to heal the sick. Through this method, the power to heal can be made available to the sick who have never even heard or read scriptures on healing. In other words, the healing power can be made available even where the Word of God has never been taught. This way or method is through manifestations of the Holy Spirit.

(Before I continue, I want to assure you that I believe the manifestations of the Holy Spirit can also be very much present where the Word *is* being preached or taught. But as I share with you one illustration of Jesus' flowing with the Holy Spirit, you will find that the power through the gifts of the Spirit was made available to people who appear to have never heard of the healing Gospel.)

### What Are the Manifestations of the Spirit?

When I speak of the manifestations of the Holy Spirit, I am speaking of what is revealed to us in First Corinthians 12:7-11.

## 1 CORINTHIANS 12:7-11

7   But the manifestation of the Spirit is given to every man to profit withal.

8   For to one is given by the Spirit the WORD OF WISDOM; to another the WORD OF KNOWLEDGE by the same Spirit;

9   To another FAITH by the same Spirit; to another the GIFTS OF HEALING by the same Spirit;

10  To another the WORKING OF MIRACLES; to another PROPHECY; to another DISCERNING OF SPIRITS; to another DIVERS KINDS OF TONGUES; to another the INTERPRETATION OF TONGUES:

11  But all these worketh that one and the selfsame Spirit, dividing to every man severally as he will.

These verses give us the names of the nine gifts of the Spirit. As the Holy Spirit works through man, these nine gifts will manifest as the Holy Spirit wills. Through the gifts of the Holy Spirit, the healing power of God can be made present even where the Word of God is not preached or taught. Any time you have a manifestation of one or more of the gifts of the Holy Spirit, the power to perform that gift accompanies the manifestation.

In the ministry of Jesus, it is very evident that Jesus ministered to the sick through two main methods: (1) through teaching and preaching the Word; and (2) through allowing the Holy Spirit to use Him as the Holy Spirit willed. Remember, the manifestations of the Holy Spirit are as *the Holy Spirit wills*, not as *we will*.

In the Gospel of John, we find a perfect example of Jesus' flowing with the Holy Spirit.

### JOHN 5:1-13

1  After this there was a feast of the Jews; and Jesus went up to Jerusalem.

2  Now there is at Jerusalem by the sheep market a pool, which is called in the Hebrew tongue Bethesda, having five porches.

3  In these lay a great multitude of impotent folk, of blind, halt, withered, waiting for the moving of the water.

4  For an angel went down at a certain season into the pool, and troubled the water: whosoever then first after the troubling of the water stepped in was made whole of whatsoever disease he had.

5  And a certain man was there, which had an infirmity thirty and eight years.

6  When Jesus saw him lie, and knew that he had been now a long time in that case, he saith unto him, Wilt thou be made whole?

7  The impotent man answered him, Sir, I have no man, when the water is troubled, to put me into the pool: but while I am coming, another steppeth down before me.

8  Jesus saith unto him, Rise, take up thy bed, and walk.

9  And immediately the man was made whole, and took up his bed, and walked: and on the same day was the sabbath.

10 The Jews therefore said unto him that was cured, It is the sabbath day: it is not lawful for thee to carry thy bed.

11 He answered them, He that made me whole, the same said unto me, Take up thy bed, and walk.

12 Then asked they him, What man is that which said unto thee, Take up thy bed, and walk?

13 And he that was healed wist not who it was: for Jesus had conveyed himself away, a multitude being in that place.

Here we have the story of Jesus at the pool of Bethesda. There are sick folk everywhere — five porches full. As Jesus steps over many sick people, you can almost hear Him saying, "Excuse Me. Excuse Me. Oops. Excuse Me. Oh, I'm sorry. Excuse Me." Jesus finally makes His way through this crowd and steps up to a man who'd had an infirmity for thirty-eight years.

Jesus speaks to the man and says "Wilt thou be made whole?" (v. 6). After the man finishes answering the question, Jesus says to him, "Rise, take up thy bed, and walk" (v. 8). At that moment, the man was healed!

As this healed man is capturing the attention of all those around him with shouts of joy and happiness, Jesus quietly turns around and says, "Excuse Me. Oops. Excuse Me" as He steps over other sick folk. In other words, Jesus left the area and went His way.

As we read this account, notice how different it is from the story of the woman with the issue of blood (Mark 5:25-34). After this woman had heard of Jesus, she "came in the press behind" and touched Jesus' garment. Jesus turned and said to her, "Daughter, thy faith hath made thee whole" (Mark 5:34).

*However, if the Holy Ghost is not moving on your behalf, you yourself can initiate obtaining the healing power by coming in contact with the Word and releasing the power within it through obedience.*

But here in John 5:1-9 we find that the individual who was healed seems to have never heard of Jesus. He didn't even know who it was who healed him. Notice John 5:13: *"And he that was healed wist not who it was: for Jesus had conveyed himself away, a multitude being in that place."* This individual did not come to Jesus for healing; Jesus came to *him*.

When the woman with the issue of blood came to Jesus, you see in her an expectation of being healed. However, this man at the pool has no expectation of *ever* getting better. John 5:6 and 7 says, *"When Jesus saw him lie, and knew that he had been now a long time in that case, he saith unto him, Wilt thou be made whole? The impotent man answered him, Sir, I have no man, when the water is troubled, to put me into the pool: but while I am coming, another steppeth down before me."*

After Jesus heard the hopelessness in this man's voice, He said to him in verse 8, "Rise, take up thy bed, and walk."

What caused Jesus to minister to this one man and pass over all the others who were also waiting for the troubling of the waters? It was a manifestation of the Holy Ghost. Jesus was *led* by the Holy Ghost to *find* this man, He was *moved on* by the Holy Ghost to *minister* to this man, and He *flowed* with the Holy Ghost to *heal* this man.

Remember what Peter said about the ministry of Jesus in Acts 10:38: *"How God anointed Jesus of Nazareth with the*

*Holy Ghost and with power: who went about doing good, and healing all that were oppressed of the devil; for God was with him."* In His ministry, Jesus not only healed through this healing power that He was given, but He also healed through flowing with the Holy Ghost. In other words, He healed through manifestations of the Holy Ghost.

Contrasting the story of the woman with the issue of blood with that of the man at the pool of Bethesda, we must come to the conclusion that in some cases, the Holy Ghost will initiate the administration of the healing power of God through one of the nine gifts.

However, if the Holy Ghost is not moving on your behalf, *you* yourself can initiate obtaining the healing power by coming in contact with the Word and releasing the power within it through obedience. Thank God, whether *God* initiates the healing process or *we* do, there is a way out from underneath the bondage of sickness and disease!

Before I conclude this chapter, a scripture in John comes to mind that I want to share with you. In John 14:12 Jesus said, *"Verily, verily, I say unto you, He that believeth on me, the works that I do shall he do also; and greater works than these shall he do; because I go unto my Father."* In order to do Jesus' works, we must know what He did! Jesus preached, taught, and He also made Himself available to the Holy Spirit to be used by Him as the Holy Spirit wills.

Notice that Jesus is not speaking to ministers in John 14:12; He is speaking to "he that believeth on Me." If you are a believer, then you are to duplicate His ministry. This means every believer should teach and preach, and every believer should make himself available to the Holy Spirit to be used as He wills.

Now I understand that all believers are not called to have a pulpit ministry. But all believers *are* called to pass on to others what they have gained through the Word and through their relationship with the Father. If we have received a glimpse of the Father's love, then we must share what we have seen with others.

Sharing and passing on what we know to others is fulfilling what Jesus said we were to do. But Jesus not only taught and proclaimed the Good News, He was also sensitive to and made Himself available to the Holy Spirit. Jesus allowed Himself to be led by the Holy Spirit, and He allowed the Holy Spirit to flow through Him as the Holy Spirit willed.

As believers today, if we only allow ourselves to teach and preach, but fail to make ourselves available to the Holy Spirit, then we will only minister at fifty percent of what is available to us. In order to reach our full potential in being a blessing to Christians and unbelievers, we must not only teach and preach, but we must be ready and available to be used by the Holy Spirit as He wills. Thank God that no matter if we are teaching or preaching the Word or flowing with the Holy Spirit, the power to destroy yokes is made available to all.

As we conclude this section, let's put ourselves in remembrance of what we have learned up to this point. The laws that govern the healing power of God include:

**1. Just because the healing power of God is present does not guarantee you will be healed.**

2. The power of the Lord can be present to heal and your senses be totally unaware of it.

3. In order to benefit from the healing power that's present, you must first *believe* that the power is present!

4. There are two ways the power of the Lord is made present to heal:

       (a) through the Word; and

       (b) through manifestations of the Holy Ghost.

# Law Number Five: The Healing Power Can Be Administered To Your Body a Number of Different Ways

Once the healing power is present, it must be administered to our bodies. It is one thing to have the healing power present; it is another thing to have the power administered to our physical bodies. In other words, the only way the healing power can *free* your body is for it to be *administered* to your body. What good would the healing power be if it was present and yet not in your body?

When it comes to a person's receiving salvation, most people agree that there is only *one* way salvation can be administered, and that is by acting on Romans 10:9: *"That if thou shalt confess with thy mouth the Lord Jesus, and shalt believe in thine heart that God hath raised him from the dead, thou shalt be saved."* The moment we confess Jesus as the Lord of our lives and believe that God has raised Him from the dead, we are saved; we obtain the saving power of God and become saved. But when it comes to obtaining the *healing* power of God, I have good news for you — there are *a number* of different ways in which the healing power may be administered to your body!

Now as I list the methods by which the healing power may be administered, I want you to be aware of the fact that I am not listing them in the order of their importance. In fact, I believe that the last method shared in this chapter will be the most prominent.

So I am not giving these methods in any particular order of priority. Please understand also that I am not giving a complete teaching concerning each one of the following methods. I will highlight them briefly and move on to the next method.

## Method Number One: Handkerchiefs and Aprons

**ACTS 19:11,12**

11 **And God wrought special miracles by the hands of Paul:**

12 **So that from his body were brought unto the sick handkerchiefs or aprons, and the diseases departed from them, and the evil spirits went out of them.**

According to these scriptures, something flowed from Paul's body into the handkerchiefs and aprons. When the handkerchiefs and aprons were laid on the sick people's bodies, evidently something was transmitted into their bodies that freed them from their sicknesses.

What was it that flowed from Paul into the handkerchiefs and aprons? What was it that was then transmitted from the handkerchiefs and aprons into the bodies of the sick? What was it that freed the sick from their sicknesses? It had to have been the healing power of God! So we must come to the conclusion that *one way the healing power can be administered to a sick person's body is through handkerchiefs and aprons that have been anointed with healing power.*

## Method Number Two: The Spoken Word

LUKE 7:1-10

1 Now when he had ended all his sayings in the audience of the people, he entered into Capernaum.

2 And a certain centurion's servant, who was dear unto him, was sick, and ready to die.

3 And when he heard of Jesus, he sent unto him the elders of the Jews, beseeching him that he would come and heal his servant.

4 And when they came to Jesus, they besought him instantly, saying, That he was worthy for whom he should do this:

5 For he loveth our nation, and he hath built us a synagogue.

6 Then Jesus went with them. And when he was now not far from the house, the centurion sent friends to him, saying unto him, Lord, trouble not thyself: for I am not worthy that thou shouldest enter under my roof:

7 Wherefore neither thought I myself worthy to come unto thee: but say in a word, and my servant shall be healed.

8 For I also am a man set under authority, having under me soldiers, and I say unto one, Go, and he goeth; and to

another, Come, and he cometh; and to my servant, Do this, and he doeth it.

9  When Jesus heard these things, he marvelled at him, and turned him about, and said unto the people that followed him, I say unto you, I have not found so great faith, no, not in Israel.

10  And they that were sent, returning to the house, found the servant whole that had been sick.

Most people are familiar with this wonderful story of the centurion and his sick servant. Luke tells us that this centurion had a servant who was very dear to him. This servant was sick, and his condition had deteriorated to the point that he was about to die. But then the centurion hears about Jesus, and, immediately, he sends friends to find this Jesus to see if they can persuade Him to come and heal the centurion's dear servant.

The friends search for and find Jesus in another town. They persuade Him to come and heal the servant. As Jesus and the centurion's friends are within view of the home where the servant is lying, the centurion sees them coming and sends another group of friends to Jesus with a message. The message is an unusual one: "Just speak the word only, and my servant shall be healed"!

Upon hearing these words, Jesus stops, turns to those who are following Him, and says that He has not come in contact with this kind of faith "no, not in Israel" (Luke 7:9). We are told by Luke that when the friends returned to the house, they found the servant who had been sick *completely healed*!

Now the question that we must ask is this: Did Jesus ever come in contact with the sick servant? No! Did Jesus touch him or give the centurion's friends a handkerchief or apron to be laid on the servant's body? No! Then how was the healing power of God transmitted from Jesus to the sick servant's body? It had to have been through the spoken word. I am convinced that Jesus went ahead and did what the centurion asked Him to do — speak the word only. Jesus spoke the word, and the servant was healed. Therefore, we can conclude that *the healing power of God can be spoken into a person's body*!

Read the words of Jesus in Mark 11:23.

### MARK 11:23

23 **For verily I say unto you, That whosoever shall say unto this mountain, Be thou removed, and be thou cast into the sea; and shall not doubt in his heart, but shall believe that those things which he saith shall come to pass; he shall have whatsoever he saith.**

Not only can someone *else* speak the healing power into your body in cooperation with your faith, but the Bible also teaches that as believers, we have the right to speak to our *own* mountains. We can speak to our own body and the healing power of God be administered!

### Method Number Three: The Name of Jesus

ACTS 3:1-7

1 **Now Peter and John went up together into the temple at the hour of prayer, being the ninth hour.**

2 **And a certain man lame from his mother's womb was carried, whom they laid daily at the gate of the temple which is**

called Beautiful, to ask alms of them that entered into the temple;

3 Who seeing Peter and John about to go into the temple asked an alms.

4 And Peter, fastening his eyes upon him with John, said, Look on us.

5 And he gave heed unto them, expecting to receive something of them.

6 Then Peter said, Silver and gold have I none; but such as I have give I thee: In the name of Jesus Christ of Nazareth rise up and walk.

7 And he took him by the right hand, and lifted him up: and immediately his feet and ankle bones received strength.

Verse 16 of Acts 3 says, *"And HIS NAME through faith in his name hath made this man strong, whom ye see and know: yea, the faith which is by him hath given him this perfect soundness in the presence of you all."* Peter and John administered the healing power of God to this man's body through *the use of the Name of Jesus*!

When Peter and John used the Name, they were only doing what Jesus had told them to do. Remember what Jesus told them in Mark 16:15-20.

MARK 16:15-20

15 . . .Go ye into all the world, and preach the gospel to every creature.

16 He that believeth and is baptized shall be saved; but he that believeth not shall be damned.

17 And these signs shall follow them that believe; IN MY NAME shall they cast out devils; they shall speak with new tongues;

18 They shall take up serpents; and if they drink any deadly thing, it shall not hurt them; they shall lay hands on the sick, and they shall recover.

19 So then after the Lord had spoken unto them, he was received up into heaven, and sat on the right hand of God.

20 And they went forth, and preached every where, the Lord working with them, and confirming the word with signs following. Amen.

There is such an urgent need in the Body of Christ today to be taught about the power that is in that Name. As Christians, we have been given the privilege and the right to speak and act in the Name of Jesus. When we do so, we are representing Jesus on the earth; we are doing the same things Jesus would do if He were here personally. It is very evident that Luke in the Book of Acts is revealing to us that another way the healing power of God is administered to the sick is through the Name of Jesus!

### Method Number Four: The Anointing of Oil And the Prayer of Faith

JAMES 5:14,15

14 Is any sick among you? let him call for the elders of the church; and let them pray over him, anointing him with oil in the name of the Lord:

15  And the prayer of faith shall save the sick, and the
Lord shall raise him up; and if he have committed sins,
they shall be forgiven him.

The Church has been given instructions by James that one
way to minister to fellow Christians is to anoint them with oil
and pray the prayer of faith over
them. Here we find another method by
which the healing power of God is
administered.

*The moment the sick
person is anointed
with oil, he should
consider himself set
apart for healing and
should boldly reject
sickness as it tries to
dominate his body!*

In the Old Testament, two entities
were anointed with oil: *people* and
*things*. When someone or something
was anointed, it meant that he or she
or the object to be anointed was to be
smeared with an anointing oil, thus signifying that the person
or thing was set apart by the Lord for a specific office or function. *When something was anointed, it was consecrated to a
specific function. And from that moment on, the thing anointed was not to be used for any other purpose!*

In Exodus 40, we find God giving instructions to Moses to
anoint *things*:

### EXODUS 40:9-11

9   And thou shalt take the anointing oil, and anoint the taber-
nacle, and all that is therein, and shalt hallow it, and all the
vessels thereof: and it shall be holy.

10  And thou shalt anoint the altar of the burnt offering, and all
his vessels, and sanctify the altar: and it shall be an altar
most holy.

11  And thou shalt anoint the laver and his foot, and sanctify it.

In Exodus 28, we find God telling Moses to anoint *people.* Once again, when someone is anointed, he is separated or *consecrated* to stand or function in a particular office. In the case of Aaron and his sons, it was the office of *priest.*

**EXODUS 28:41**

**41 And thou shalt put them upon Aaron thy brother, and his sons with him; and shalt anoint them, and consecrate them, and sanctify them, that they may minister unto me in the priest's office.**

Now in the New Testament, when James tells us to anoint a sick person with oil, I am convinced that the person anointed should consider himself set apart or *consecrated* for healing and should not accept anything less. If the anointed laver or altar in the Old Testament was not to be used for anything other than service to the Lord after the anointing with oil took place, then why should we allow our bodies to be used for anything other than healing once *we* have been anointed with oil?

*The moment the sick person is anointed with oil, he should consider himself set apart for healing and should boldly reject sickness as it tries to dominate his body!*

If we are going to use the anointing of oil as a method of obtaining the healing power, we should instruct the recipients before we do so, and they must understand the significance of this act. People who have been anointed with oil should think differently about themselves from that moment on. They should see themselves set apart for healing!

## What To Expect After the Prayer of Faith Is Prayed

Notice also in James 5 that James not only tells the Church to anoint the sick with oil but also *to pray the prayer of faith* for them. What is this prayer of faith? What should the sick expect to happen when this prayer is prayed?

The prayer of faith is found in Mark 11:24, which says, *"Therefore I say unto you, What things soever ye desire, when ye pray, believe that ye receive them, and ye shall have them."* The prayer of faith is a prayer that receives something whenever it is used. Jesus said that when we pray this prayer, we are to "believe that we receive."

What are we to believe we receive when we have been anointed with oil and prayed for? We are to believe that we receive the healing power of God! This is the reason that the anointing of oil and the prayer of faith is another method by which the healing power of God can be administered to a fellow Christian's sick body.

### Method Number Five:
### Praying the Prayer of Faith for Yourself

As I discussed briefly, the prayer of faith can be found in Mark 11:24: *"Therefore I say unto you, What things soever ye desire, when ye pray, believe that ye receive them, and ye shall have them."* And as I stated in the previous method of obtaining God's healing power, the prayer of faith can be used by elders when they have been called to pray for a fellow Christian.

But the prayer of faith can also be used by an individual for himself. A sick person may pray this prayer for himself in the privacy of his own home. It is another method of obtaining healing power. Jesus instructed those who used this method to believe they receive *when they pray*. Therefore, it is very evident that when we pray, we will receive something. However, we must *believe* that we receive it *when* we pray.

The word "receive" means *to take*. When we pray and ask for healing, *at that moment,* we are to believe that we have taken it. Taken what? Received what? The healing power of God that has been supplied to us through the death, burial, and resurrection of Jesus!

So many are using this prayer of faith, but unless they see healing manifested in their bodies, they refuse to come to the conclusion that they received. But Jesus did not instruct us to wait until we see changes in our body and *then* believe we receive. Jesus said that *when we pray,* we are to believe that we receive. Once we believe we receive, what is there left to do but to give thanks to the One who gave the healing power of God to us when we prayed?

Once you believe you receive, spend time thanking God that the healing power is working in you to drive out sickness or disease!

If we would follow the instructions of Mark 11:24, the moment we prayed and believed we received, we would cease trying to *get* God to heal us. Why? Because we believed we received the healing power of God that's already been made available to us. Thank God for different methods by which the healing power of God can be administered to our bodies!

## Method Number Six: The Laying on of Hands

In the ministry of Jesus, which is revealed to us through the Gospels, we find one particular method by which Jesus ministered healing power to the sick. The method Jesus used above all other methods was the laying on of hands. It is one way that the healing power of God is administered to our physical bodies.

The following scriptures show Jesus using this method of the laying on of hands to minister healing power to people.

### MARK 8:22-25

22 And he cometh to Bethsaida; and they bring a blind man unto him, and besought him to touch him.

23 And he took the blind man by the hand, and led him out of the town; and when he had spit on his eyes, AND PUT HIS HANDS UPON HIM, he asked him if he saw ought.

24 And he looked up, and said, I see men as trees, walking.

25 After that HE PUT HIS HANDS AGAIN UPON HIS EYES, and made him look up: and he was restored, and saw every man clearly.

### MARK 6:1-6

1 And he went out from thence, and came into his own country; and his disciples follow him.

2 And when the sabbath day was come, he began to teach in the synagogue: and many hearing him were astonished, saying, From whence hath this man these things? and what wisdom is this which is given unto him, that even such mighty works are wrought by his hands?

3 Is not this the carpenter, the son of Mary, the brother of James, and Joses, and of Juda, and Simon? and are not his sisters here with us? And they were offended at him.

4 But Jesus said unto them, A prophet is not without honour, but in his own country, and among his own kin, and in his own house.

5 And he could there do no mighty work, save that HE LAID HIS HANDS UPON A FEW SICK FOLK, and healed them.

6 And he marvelled because of their unbelief. And he went round about the villages, teaching.

### LUKE 4:40

40 Now when the sun was setting, all they that had any sick with divers diseases brought them unto him; and HE LAID HIS HANDS ON EVERY ONE OF THEM, and healed them.

Jesus believed so much in this method of ministering to the sick that He commissioned every believer to use this same method. Remember what Jesus said in Mark 16.

### MARK 16:15-18

15 And he said unto them, Go ye into all the world, and preach the gospel to every creature.

16 He that believeth and is baptized shall be saved; but he that believeth not shall be damned.

17 And these signs shall follow them that believe; In my name shall they cast out devils; they shall speak with new tongues;

**18 They shall take up serpents; and if they drink any deadly thing, it shall not hurt them; THEY SHALL LAY HANDS ON THE SICK, and they shall recover.**

Jesus said, *". . .they shall lay hands on the sick, and they shall recover."* What begins the recovery process is the administration of the healing power through the laying on of hands! It's impossible to begin to recover if the healing power has not been administered first. The instant hands are laid on us, from that moment on, we should consider ourselves to be recovering because the healing power is in us working mightily!

I have given you a brief description of the methods through which the healing power is administered to our bodies: *handkerchiefs and aprons*; *the spoken word*; *anointing of oil and the prayer of faith*; *praying the prayer of faith yourself*; *the Name of Jesus*; and *the laying on of hands*.

I am personally convinced that the laying on of hands will be the predominant way most Christians will receive the healing

> *The instant hands are laid on us, from that moment on, we should consider ourselves to be recovering because the healing power is in us working mightily!*

power of God. Another way we could say that is, most Christians are going to be able to *comprehend* better that the healing power of God was administered to their bodies after hands were laid on them than through the use of any other method. Most people can believe more easily that something was administered to their body when they were touched by a hand than they can believe that healing power was administered when a handkerchief or apron was placed upon them.

I'll say it another way: It is easier for people to comprehend that something is given to them when hands are laid on them than if someone were to just walk up to them and say, "Be healed!" For some reason, most do not have the comprehension that something can be administered to them through the spoken word.

## The Laying On of Hands
## Is a Basic Bible Doctrine

Why do I believe that the laying on of hands will be the predominant way for most Christians to receive the healing power of God? Because the Book of Hebrews tells me that the doctrine of laying on of hands is referred to as the milk of the Word.

### HEBREWS 5:12-14

12  For when for the time ye ought to be teachers, ye have need that one teach you again which be the first principles of the oracles of God; and are become such as have need of milk, and not of strong meat.

13  For every one that useth milk is unskilful in the word of righteousness: for he is a babe.

14  But strong meat belongeth to them that are of full age, even those who by reason of use have their senses exercised to discern both good and evil.

### HEBREWS 6:1,2

1  Therefore leaving the principles of the doctrine of Christ, let us go on unto perfection; not laying again the foundation of repentance from dead works, and of faith toward God,

**2 Of the doctrine of baptisms, and of laying on of hands, and of resurrection of the dead, and of eternal judgment.**

Paul tells us that "repentance from dead works" is "milk," and the message "of faith toward God" is "milk" too. The milk of the Word is also the "doctrine of baptisms," the "doctrine of laying on of hands," and so forth.

We understand that the milk of the Word is referring to areas that young Christians should be taught about when they enter Christianity. It is also referring to areas that young Christians can receive and benefit from the quickest. It is easier for young Christians to *comprehend* that the healing power of God is administered to their bodies after they have had hands laid on them than through the use of any other method. There is something about the laying on of hands that people can accept the fact that something was given to them the moment hands are laid on them.

There is a very interesting record of something that happened to Jesus in His own hometown. It is found in the sixth chapter of the Book of Mark. Mark tells us that Jesus went into His hometown, taught them, and tried to set them free from their sicknesses. But Mark gives us a very sad commentary about His success. Mark tells us that Jesus "...*could there do no mighty work, save that he laid his hands upon a few sick folk, and healed them*" (Mark 6:5).

(We're talking about the fact that most Christians will be able to believe quicker that healing power is administered to them when hands are laid on them than if that power is administered to them through any other method. This is due to the fact that the laying on of hands is the milk of the Word.)

It appears that Mark is telling us in Mark 6:5 that when no other method of administering healing power would be accepted, some of these people in Jesus' hometown did allow Him to lay His hands upon them for healing. It appears that the laying on of hands worked when nothing else would! You might ask, "What do you mean by 'nothing else'?" When speaking healing into their bodies would not be accepted, Jesus could lay hands on a few sick folks. When the anointing of oil and the prayer of faith would not be permitted, He could lay hands on some of the people. The laying on of hands will work when other methods will not be accepted!

## Old Testament Examples
## Of the Laying On of Hands To Confer Something

In Old Testament times, people believed in the laying on of hands. They would actually take a goat, lay their hands on it, confess all the sins of the camp onto the goat, and then release the goat into the wilderness to be judged. We are told of this practice in Leviticus 16.

### LEVITICUS 16:21,22

21 And Aaron shall lay both his hands upon the head of the live goat, and confess over him all the iniquities of the children of Israel, and all their transgressions in all their sins, putting them upon the head of the goat, and shall send him away by the hand of a fit man into the wilderness:

22 And the goat shall bear upon him all their iniquities unto a land not inhabited: and he shall let go the goat in the wilderness.

These people believed that the sins of the people would be transmitted to the goat through the laying on of the hands of the priest. They believed in the laying on of hands!

In the Old Testament, we also see fathers on their deathbeds calling their children to their bedside. They would then take each child, lay their hands upon him, and pronounce blessings upon him. These people believed in the laying on of hands!

An example of the laying on of hands to confer blessings is found in Genesis 48 when Joseph, knowing that his father would not live much longer, brings his two sons to his father to be blessed.

**GENESIS 48:13-20**

13  And Joseph took them both, Ephraim in his right hand toward Israel's left hand, and Manasseh in his left hand toward Israel's right hand, and brought them near unto him.

14  And Israel stretched out his right hand, and laid it upon Ephraim's head, who was the younger, and his left hand upon Manasseh's head, guiding his hands wittingly; for Manasseh was the firstborn.

15  And he blessed Joseph, and said, God, before whom my fathers Abraham and Isaac did walk, the God which fed me all my life long unto this day,

16  The Angel which redeemed me from all evil, bless the lads; and let my name be named on them, and the name of my fathers Abraham and Isaac; and let them grow into a multitude in the midst of the earth.

17 And when Joseph saw that his father laid his right hand upon the head of Ephraim, it displeased him: and he held up his father's hand, to remove it from Ephraim's head unto Manasseh's head.

18 And Joseph said unto his father, Not so, my father: for this is the firstborn; put thy right hand upon his head.

19 And his father refused, and said, I know it, my son, I know it; he also shall become a people, and he also shall be great: but truly his younger brother shall be greater than he, and his seed shall become a multitude of nations.

20 And he blessed them that day, saying, In thee shall Israel bless, saying, God make thee as Ephraim and as Manasseh: and he set Ephraim before Manasseh.

Can you see that these Old Testament saints believed in the laying on of hands for the purpose of transmitting blessings?

In the New Testament, we see again and again people coming to Jesus and beseeching Him to come and *lay His hands on* the sick. Their requests reveal their belief that when hands were laid on the sick, something happened. What happened? Healing power was administered! *Glory!*

This understanding that power is administered through the laying on of hands — if it is embraced by the sick — would eliminate so much worry and fear concerning whether or not they are going to recover. If the sick believed that the same healing power went into them when hands were laid upon them that went into the woman with the issue of blood, then they could release a sigh of relief. In their thoughts would be the words, *Glory! The healing power of God is working in my body to drive out sickness!* They would say, "I know the healing power of God is in my body, because I had hands laid on me according to Mark 16:18, which says, '. . .*they shall lay hands on the sick, and they shall recover.*'"

Now that I have made you aware of the methods by which the Bible reveals to us that the healing power is administered, I can boldly make this statement: In order to be set free from sickness and disease, you must first come into contact with one of the following methods. If you have not had a handkerchief or apron laid on you; if you or someone else hasn't spoken the healing power of God into your body; if you haven't called for the elders and had them anoint you with oil and pray the prayer of faith; if you haven't prayed the prayer of faith for yourself; if you haven't had the Name of Jesus spoken over you; or if you haven't had hands laid on you — *then you are not going to be healed.*

These methods are God's means by which He can get to you the healing power that is necessary to destroy the yoke of sickness in your body. The healing power of God must be administered to your body through one of these methods.

Now you understand that when the Holy Ghost manifests Himself through one of the nine gifts listed in First Corinthians 12:8-10, He will also use one of these methods to administer healing power into your body. For example, many times I have called out a particular disease through a word of knowledge during a church service. Instead of calling those who responded to come forward to lay my hands on them, I have simply spoken to them by saying, "Be healed." The instant I spoke those words to them, I am convinced that the healing power of God was immediately administered to their bodies. *Glory!*

Some may ask, "Which method should I use in order to have the healing power administered to my body?" I suggest that you use the method that you believe in the strongest. Find a method that you do have some confidence in; then connect _your_ faith with _His_ power!

# 9 chapter

## Law Number Six: When the Healing Power of God Is Administered, You Might or Might *Not* Feel It!

Many ministers feel the healing power of God go out of their hands when they are ministering to the sick. On the other side of the coin, I have spoken to many ministers who've said they feel *nothing* when they are ministering to the sick.

Also, when speaking to people who have been ministered to, I have had many of them tell me that they felt something when they were ministered to. Yet I have had as many tell me that they felt nothing. Some have even expressed to me their belief that since they did not feel anything when hands were laid upon them, they must not have received anything. But that is simply not true.

## Feeling the Power Will Be
## The Exception, Not the Rule

I believe it is possible for a minister to feel the healing power going out of his hands, and I also believe it is possible for the *recipient* of the healing power to feel the power being administered. However, I must say that it will be the exception rather than the rule. I do not believe that a minister *must* feel the healing power go out of his hands to be convinced that it did. I also do not believe that the recipient *must* feel the power go into him before he can believe that it was administered. If a person had to wait until he felt the power go into him in order to believe that it was administered, he would be walking by feelings and not by faith.

There is one scriptural record of Jesus' feeling the power go out of Him, and in the same record, the recipient also felt the power being administered. This record is found in Mark 5:25-34. We know it as the story of the woman with the issue of blood.

### MARK 5:25-34

25 And a certain woman, which had an issue of blood twelve years,

26 And had suffered many things of many physicians, and had spent all that she had, and was nothing bettered, but rather grew worse,

27 When she had heard of Jesus, came in the press behind, and touched his garment.

28 For she said, If I may touch but his clothes, I shall be whole.

29 And straightway the fountain of her blood was dried up; and SHE FELT IN HER BODY that she was healed of that plague.

30 And Jesus, immediately KNOWING IN HIMSELF THAT VIRTUE HAD GONE OUT OF HIM, turned him about in the press, and said, Who touched my clothes?

31 And his disciples said unto him, Thou seest the multitude thronging thee, and sayest thou, Who touched me?

32 And he looked round about to see her that had done this thing.

33 But the woman fearing and trembling, knowing what was done in her, came and fell down before him, and told him all the truth.

34 And he said unto her, Daughter, thy faith hath made thee whole; go in peace, and be whole of thy plague.

Notice as you read verse 30 that it is evident that Jesus felt that virtue or power flow out of Him. It is also evident that the woman felt that power enter into her (verse 29).

I was reading this account one day when, suddenly, it dawned on me that this is the only account from the healings of Jesus in which there is any mention of His feeling the power go out from Him. This alone tells me that it is possible for a minister to feel the power going out of him when ministering to the sick. But it's going to be the exception rather than the rule. If it were to be the norm, then there would be mention of Jesus' feeling the power go out of Him every time He touched someone to minister to him or her, but there is not.

Once I saw this, it settled a lingering question for me personally. Therefore, I am going to continue to lay hands on the
sick whether I feel the power go out of my hands or not. I am
going to believe that the healing power of God is ministered to
the sick every time I touch them. Whether I feel something or
not, I choose to believe Mark 16:18, which says, *"They shall
take up serpents; and if they drink any deadly thing, it shall not
hurt them; THEY SHALL LAY HANDS ON THE SICK, AND
THEY SHALL RECOVER."*

Those who are being ministered to should take the same
position. Yes, we have the example of the woman in Mark 5,
who apparently felt something when she touched Jesus. But,
remember, in all the other healings found in the Gospels, we
find no other record of any sick person feeling anything when
he was ministered to by Jesus. Therefore, we must come to the
conclusion that whether we feel anything or not, when hands
are laid on us, we must believe that the healing power of God is
being administered to our bodies. Remember we are to walk by
faith and not by what we feel.

I remember in the late seventies, it seemed everyone was
falling out onto the floor under the power of God when hands
were laid upon them for healing. I'd have people say to me, "I
didn't fall. Does that mean I didn't receive?" My response was
always the same, "No, falling or not falling does not determine
who gets healed and who doesn't." Nowhere in the Bible does it
say you have to fall in order to get healed. And nowhere in the
Bible does it say you have to feel the power go into you before
you can begin to believe that it has been administered.

In order for me to believe that the healing power is in my
body, I must ask myself one question: "Have I had hands laid
on me for healing?" If the answer to this question is yes, then I

can conclude that the power is present in my body. If I've had the elders of my church come and anoint me with oil and pray the prayer of faith, then the power is in me. Or if I have spoken to my body and commanded it to be well, then the power is in me. Thank God for the truth of His Word that sets us free from being controlled by what we feel or see!

# 10 chapter

## Law Number Seven:
### The Healing Power of God Can Be in You And Yet Lie Within You Inactive

If you have ever had the opportunity of attending one of Rev. Kenneth E. Hagin's crusades where he is ministering to the sick, you have heard him say something like this: "The moment I lay my hands upon you, the healing power of God will be administered to your body. But what you do with it after that is up to you." The following chapters are dedicated to teaching you what *you* must do with the power once it is administered to you. You have a part to play if the power is going to manifest healing in your body once it has been administered.

People who have had the healing power administered to their body through one of the methods mentioned in Law

Number Five (Chapter 8) must be aware of the fact that the power has the ability to lie within them dormant or inactive. In other words, just because the healing power is administered to their body does not guarantee that they will be healed.

For example, I know of people who have been called into the ministry, maybe to the office of pastor or teacher, yet they have never done anything with it; they have never answered the call. They have never gone into the ministry. Question: Is the call of God still on their life? Yes, the Bible says the gifts and calling of God are without repentance (Rom. 11:29). Once my Heavenly Father has called a person to a ministry office, He will never take that calling from that individual.

Understanding this means that a person can have a call upon his life, and yet that call can lie within him dormant or inactive. A call that is upon a person's life does not manifest itself just because it is present. *So it is with the healing power.* It can be present in your body and yet lie dormant or inactive. It does not manifest itself in your body just because it has been administered to your body.

First Timothy 4:14 says, *"Neglect not the gift that is in thee, which was given thee by prophecy, with the laying on of the hands of the presbytery."* Here we find Paul encouraging Timothy concerning something that God had given to him. Paul called what was given to Timothy a *gift*. The vehicle God used to get this gift to Timothy was the laying on of hands. What this gift was is unclear, but what *is* clear is that Paul told Timothy not to neglect it.

The word "neglect" means *to ignore* or *to be careless of*. With this word "neglect," Paul is implying that Timothy has not given this gift the proper attention, and, therefore, Timothy has caused this gift to lie within him dormant or inactive. Paul implies that this neglected, ignored gift will produce nothing in or through Timothy's life until he stops neglecting it.

Now I understand that what Paul is speaking about in this verse is not the healing power. Yet this verse does support the truth that a person can have something given to him through the laying on of hands and the thing given lie dormant or inactive until the person who received it does something with it.

### You Must Keep the Gift Active Within You

Too many people have the mistaken idea that once a gift has been given to someone by God, God will be the one who makes sure the gift keeps working until it is able to manifest itself in or through that person. But do you see Paul telling Timothy in First Timothy 4 that God is the one who is supposed to keep the gift from becoming dormant or inactive? No, Paul gives _Timothy_ the responsibility of keeping the gift active and working. Also, do you understand that the gift does not have the power in and of itself to keep working? The gift neglected will become dormant or inactive.

_We are the ones who have been given the responsibility of keeping what God gives us active and working by refusing to neglect it, ignore it, or be careless of it._

We must understand that when God gives us something, _He_ is not responsible to keep it working, and _the gift_ is not responsible to keep itself working. _We_ are the ones who have been given the responsibility of keeping what God gives us active and working by refusing to _neglect it, ignore it,_ or _be careless of it._ Many who have need of healing will never benefit from the healing power of God that is in them until they learn how to give the power the proper attention needed for it to continue to work in them once it has been obtained.

Second Timothy 1:6 says, *"Wherefore I put thee in remembrance that thou stir up the gift of God, which is in thee by the putting on of my hands."* Here is the second time Paul talks to Timothy about this gift that Timothy had been given through the laying on of hands. (I have found it necessary to remind people more than once, too, of the healing power that is in them. People have a tendency to get so taken up with the problem that they forget about what has been given to them through the laying on of hands.)

This time, in Second Timothy 1:6, Paul uses a stronger phrase than he did in First Timothy 4:14. Instead of saying, "Do not neglect the gift," this time he says, "Stir up the gift." Timothy is told that the gift within him needs to be stirred up.

Now notice Paul did not tell Timothy to pray and ask God to stir up the gift that was inside him. No, once God gives you something, it is yours from that point on. And what you do with it is up to you, not God. If you neglect it, ignore it, or fail to stir it up, there is nothing that God can do to cause the gift to be active and productive within you.

To illustrate this point, if I gave you a watch as a gift, then from that instant, it would be your responsibility, not mine, to keep that watch running. What you do with the watch after it has been given to you is up to you. So it is with the healing power of God. It will be given to you the instant hands are laid on you. But from that moment, what you do with it is up to you. You can neglect it, ignore it, be careless of it, and fail to stir it up. Or you can stir it up and give it the proper attention, and see it produce in you what God planned all along — *healing*!

Paul told Timothy to *". . .stir up the gift of God, which is in thee by the putting on of my hands"* (2 Tim. 1:6). This phrase "stir up" implies *to arouse from dormancy.* Here again, we find this truth that what was given to Timothy was lying inactive or dormant. It is very evident that the gift that was given to Timothy was still in him even though it was dormant. The gift did not leave Timothy just because he did not keep it active after it was received.

It is also very evident that the gift could have been stirred up or aroused from dormancy anytime Timothy desired. If Timothy wanted to wait three weeks, three months, or three years, the gift would still be lying within him dormant, waiting for him to stir it up.

### The Healing Power May Lie Dormant, But It Will Not Go Away

Likewise, the healing power of God will lie within us dormant until we choose to stir it up. It does not evaporate or dissipate after a certain period of time. For example, if you had a kidney problem five years ago and had hands laid on you five years ago for healing, the instant hands were laid on you, the healing power of God was administered to your kidneys. But as the days passed, if you ignored or neglected the power that was administered, the healing power would still be present. Five years later, that same healing power would still be present in your kidneys! It would not leave, but it would be lying dormant within you.

If we choose to allow the healing power to remain inactive in us once it has been administered to our bodies, then we will continue to be dominated by sickness. But the instant we stir the healing power up, we make it active, and it begins to drive out the sickness and to recover our bodies from the sickened condition. We must learn not to neglect what has been given to us!

Another example of something that has been given to us by God and yet has the capability of lying dormant or inactive is the ability to walk in love toward others. Romans 5:5 says, *"And hope maketh not ashamed; because the love of God is shed abroad in our hearts by the Holy Ghost which is given unto us."*

I know people who are born again, who have had the love of God shed abroad in their hearts by the Holy Ghost, and yet you never see any evidence of this love. They have the ability to walk in love; they have the ability to forgive. Yet they do not forgive; they do not walk in love toward others. But the ability to walk in love never "evaporates" — it will never leave you. Once God has given it to you, it is yours for life.

*One reason people neglect and fail to stir up the healing power given when hands are laid upon them is, they are unaware that it is given to them when hands are laid upon them.*

This is solid evidence that a Christian can be given something from God and yet what has been given can lie dormant or inactive. So many are allowing the love of God to lie dormant within them.

Now we understand that every born-again child of God has the ability to stir up this love that is within him anytime he chooses. Remember, once God gives you the ability to walk in love, what you do with it afterward is up to you, not God. If God could stir up the love in you and cause it to become active,

I am sure He would be doing it daily. But we must understand that as much as God desires for you to walk in love, He cannot force love to become active in you. You are the only one who controls whether love is dormant or active in your life.

If you can have love lying within you dormant — if you can have a call to the ministry lying within you inactive — then it is possible to have the healing power in you and *it* lie within you inactive. So many have the mistaken idea that if the healing power has been administered, then they are guaranteed to be healed. This is untrue. If it were true, then if you have a call of God upon your life, you would just go into the ministry automatically whether you wanted to or not. Or if you have the love of God in you, then you are guaranteed to walk in love every day of your life whether you wanted to or not.

No, the call does not dictate what you will do in life. The love does not force you to walk in love. And the healing power does not heal you just because it is present. You have a part to play. If you do not play your part, these things will lie within you dormant or inactive.

This same principle is true when we use First John 1:9 which says, "If we confess our sins, he is faithful and just to forgive us our sins, and to cleanse us from all unrighteousness." The instant we confess a sin to the Father, He forgives us. In other words, we receive forgiveness. Then two hours later, suppose we start to be dominated by feelings of inferiority and guilt about the very thing we asked forgiveness for. We begin to walk governed by our feelings, and for the next two days, we conclude that God did not forgive us when we asked Him to.

Then later while in church, our pastor is preaching, and we suddenly realize that we were forgiven the moment we asked two days ago. We realize that our feelings have been lying to us ever since! While we are sitting in that church service, we speak up on the inside and say, Wait a minute. My Father said that if I would confess my sins, He would forgive me. I confessed; there-fore, in spite of what my feelings are saying to me, I believe that I have been forgiven. I was forgiven two days ago. I stir up that which I have allowed to become dormant within me. I stir up the forgiveness I received two days ago.

*Another reason why people neglect and fail to stir up the healing power when hands are laid on them is, their attention is fixed on their problem.*

From that point on, we will begin to benefit from the very forgiveness that we received two days earlier. This forgiveness was lying within us dormant — inactive — for two days! The forgiveness did not go away. It had been administered to us the instant we asked, but it lay within us dormant until we stirred it up and began to reap the benefits of it.

### Activate That Which God Has Given To You!

You can stir up the call on your life anytime you want to if the call is present. If you are born again, you can stir up the love of God and walk in love anytime you want to. And if you have had the healing power administered to your body, you can stir up the healing power of God anytime you desire.

The gift or call of God will lie within you until you decide to do something with it. I know certain Christians to whom I would like to say, "Would you please arouse from dormancy that call of God upon your life?" I know some Christians to whom I would like to say, "Would you please arouse the love of God that has been shed abroad in your heart by the Holy

Ghost? Would you stir it up, *please*? It's in there sleeping!" I'm sure you know what I'm talking about!

I wonder how many good people have failed to receive their manifestations of healing (and have blamed God for not giving them healing) based on their body's never being freed from the sickness. In other words, they allowed the healing power to lie dormant within them simply because they didn't see or feel the desired results in their body. So many of us have failed, not because *God* did not do anything when we were prayed for but, rather, because *we* allowed the healing power that was given to us to lie dormant within us!

It's time we began to understand that spiritual things can lie within us dormant until two things happen: (1) *we become aware of their presence*; and (2) *we take upon ourselves the responsibility of stirring up what we have been given.*

Failure to become aware of and to activate what God has given us will cause us to fail to benefit from it completely. There are so many sick ones to whom God has given healing power through the laying on of hands, who will continue to suffer because they are either totally unaware of the power's presence or they fail to keep it active once it has been received.

There are reasons why people neglect the healing power; there are reasons why people fail to stir up the healing power and allow it to lie within them dormant. One reason people neglect and fail to stir up the healing power given when hands are laid upon them is, they *are unaware that it is given to them when hands are laid upon them.*

How often have I seen people enter prayer lines, have hands laid on them, and then on the way back to their seats, check to see if anything has happened in their bodies! They are checking to see if God has given them anything. So when they still feel the problem in their bodies, they come to the quick conclusion that God didn't do anything for them, and they leave another healing service disappointed.

*It's one thing for the healing power of God to be made available to us through Jesus, but it is another thing altogether to have that power administered to our bodies.*

These types of people are completely unaware of the healing power that was administered to their bodies. Because they are unaware of the power's presence, they allow it to become dormant or inactive.

These types of people will have to be convinced that the power was given to them when hands were laid on them. They will have to be convinced of its presence before you could begin to talk to them about stirring that power up.

It's easy to identify those who are unaware that the healing power has been administered to their bodies. They are recognized by their words. For example, people who say things such as, "God's going to heal me; God's going to do it" reveal that they do not believe that when they were prayed for, God gave them healing power. What a sad opinion of God they have.

Listen to the sick confess scriptures concerning healing. I have heard people confess things such as, "I believe that by the stripes of Jesus I am healed." I have heard confessions such as, "Jesus took my infirmities and bore my sicknesses." These truths are from the Bible, all right, but what I like to listen for is the *attitude* with which the truths were spoken. What I have found is that the majority of people who confess such things have the mentality that Jesus provided — *supplied* — healing for them. They have the mentality that through His death, burial, and resurrection, Jesus made healing available to them. Yet they show no evidence that they are aware of the fact that the healing power that Jesus supplied to them through His death was administered to their bodies when they were prayed for.

It's one thing for the healing power of God to be made *available* to us through Jesus, but it is another thing altogether to have that power *administered* to our bodies. People who believe that the healing power has been administered to their bodies will think and talk differently than those who only believe that Jesus supplied the healing power through His death.

The same point can be made using the subject of salvation. I know sinners who believe that Jesus died for their sins, yet they have never asked Jesus into their hearts. Jesus' *supplying* salvation and the sinner's *receiving* salvation into his life are two entirely different things.

Mark 11:24 says, *"Therefore I say unto you, What things soever ye desire, when ye pray, believe that ye receive them, and ye shall have them."* In this scripture, Jesus did not tell us to believe that healing was supplied to us. He said to "believe that you receive."

There is a huge difference between believing that Jesus supplied healing and believing that the healing power was received into your body when you were prayed for.

As I said, one way to determine whether or not people are aware of the fact that the healing power has been administered to their bodies is by listening to them. You can recognize by their words whether or not they are aware that healing power has been administered to them.

Remember, we are talking about the reasons why people neglect the healing power — why they fail to stir up the healing power. We said that one reason why they neglect and fail to stir it up is, when hands are laid on them, *they are unaware that the power was given to them at the time hands were laid on them.*

Another reason why people neglect and fail to stir up the healing power when hands are laid on them is, *their attention is fixed on their problem.*

The word "neglect" means *to ignore* or *to be careless of.* It implies that you have your attention on other things.

One of the main reasons people neglect the healing power of God is due to their attention being fixed on their problem. For example, you know you are neglecting the healing power of God when the only thing you can think about is the doctor's report. When the only thing you can see with your mind's eye is the image on the X-ray, you know that's a good indicator that you are guilty of neglecting the healing power of God.

Problems can and will demand our attention, but we must not allow them to cause us to neglect the very thing that will destroy the yoke off of us.

Neglected power is *dormant* power.

Neglected power is *inactive* power.

Neglected power is *idle* power.

We cannot afford to allow our attention to become so distracted by our problems that we find ourselves guilty of neglecting the healing power of God within us. Since we are not to neglect it, then what must we do to place the proper amount of attention upon it so that it will destroy the yoke of sickness in our bodies? Paul tells us the answer in his instructions to Timothy in First Timothy 4:14 and 15.

## How To Stir Up What Is Within You!

### 1 TIMOTHY 4:14,15

14 Neglect not the gift that is in thee, which was given thee by prophecy, with the laying on of the hands of the presbytery.

15 Meditate upon these things; give thyself wholly to them; that thy profiting may appear to all.

Meditation and giving yourself wholly to the gift received are the means by which we keep ourselves from neglecting the gift. Timothy was told to do these two things after the gift had been given to him. He was *not* told to do these two things in order to *obtain* this gift. Therefore, these two areas — meditation and giving yourself wholly to it — are things that we are to do *after* we have received the healing power.

Too many have the idea that once the power has been received, then the work is all over. They believe that they no longer have to think about this power — they no longer have to talk about this power. This idea is far from the truth.

Timothy was told to do two things concerning the gift that had been given him through the laying on of hands: He was to *meditate upon it,* and he was to *give himself wholly* to the gift received. It would be impossible for the gift to be neglected and lie dormant as long as Timothy followed Paul's instructions.

If we are to keep the healing power of God active in our lives, we must follow the same instructions given to Timothy by Paul. The instructions to "meditate" and to "give yourself wholly" must be applied to the healing power within you. Doing so will ensure that the power is kept working in you until you are satisfied with the fruit produced. Doing so will cause you not to neglect the gift.

## Think, Talk, and Give Thanks

Therefore, if you are told to meditate on what has been given to you through the laying on of hands, then *meditate!* When you meditate on something, you *ponder* it; you *think* about it. Therefore, spend time *thinking* about how Jesus supplied this healing power through His death, burial, and resurrection. Spend time *thinking* about the method by which the power was administered to your body. Spend time *thinking* about what the healing power is doing within you now. If you are not thinking about these three things, then you are not meditating on the gift of the healing power given you through the laying on of hands, and the healing power will lie within you dormant. It's that simple.

*It's one thing for the healing power of God to be made available to us through Jesus, but it is another thing altogether to have that power administered to our bodies.*

The second thing Paul told Timothy to do was to "give himself wholly" to the gift given. "Giving yourself wholly" to something means that you *dedicate yourself to what has been given.* Your attention is *fixed* on what has been given. The thing you give yourself wholly to will captivate your attention so deeply that if I give you half a chance, you will tell me everything you have discovered about that thing. Things you have given yourself wholly to will thrill you to think about, read about, talk about, and share with others about. Things you give yourself wholly to will give you so much pleasure that you wish everyone you meet would also obtain and enjoy what you have given yourself wholly to.

Therefore, proof that you have given yourself wholly to something will be revealed through your *words* and *actions*. I can determine what you have given yourself wholly to by observing these two areas in your life.

*What you have given yourself wholly to will eventually appear unto all!*

If we are to give ourselves wholly to what has been given, then we must fix our attention on the healing power of God. Spend time *talking* about how Jesus supplied this healing power through His death, burial, and resurrection. Spend time *talking* about the method by which the power was administered to your body. Spend time *talking* about what the healing power is doing within you now.

When we have so given ourselves to these truths, they will so thrill our hearts that the only thing left to do is to spend time *thanking* our Heavenly Father who made the healing power available to us through the sacrifice of His Son Jesus! Spend time *thanking* Him for making you aware of the methods by which the power was administered to your body. Spend time *thanking* Him for supplying such mighty power that no sickness can stand against it and remain in your body. When the power encounters sickness, sickness is the loser every time! Praise God! Spend time *thanking* God because the power is working mightily in you, recovering your body from any sickened condition.

Every time the enemy comes and begins to raise questions in your mind concerning whether or not the power is in you, respond to his negative thoughts with a bold declaration. Tell him out loud how Jesus supplied the healing power through His death, burial, and resurrection. With your mouth, inform the enemy how the healing power was administered to your body. Then declare with confidence what the healing power is doing in you now, recovering your body from the sickened condition. By doing this, you will successfully resist him every time. Remember what James 4:7 says: *"Submit yourselves therefore to God. Resist the devil, and he will flee from you."*

Refuse to allow the healing power of God to lie dormant within you! If you stop *thinking*, *talking*, and *thanking* concerning the healing power of God in you, you will be guilty of neglecting the power and allowing it to become dormant.

It's kind of like a marriage. If you stop *thinking* about your spouse, if you stop *talking* to and about your spouse, if you stop *thanking* your Heavenly Father for your spouse, your marriage relationship will become neglected. But you can arouse your marriage from dormancy by *thinking* about and *talking* to and about your spouse and by *thanking* the Father for your spouse.

First Timothy 4:14 and 15 says, *"Neglect not the gift that is in thee, which was given thee by prophecy, with the laying on of the hands of the presbytery. MEDITATE upon these things; GIVE THYSELF WHOLLY TO THEM; that thy profiting may appear to all."* Paul gave Timothy the instructions to meditate and to give himself wholly to the gift given for a purpose. The purpose of these instructions is found in the phrase *". . .that thy profiting may appear to all."* When did Timothy originally profit? *When hands were laid upon him and he was given this gift.*

But Paul told Timothy that his profiting — the gift — would never appear to all unless he meditated upon it and gave himself wholly to it. Paul told Timothy if he neglected this gift — if he ignored it or was careless of it — it would *not* appear to all. Should Timothy have chosen not to obey the instructions to meditate and give himself wholly to the gift, then no one around him would have ever known that he had received something through the laying on of hands. His mother would have never known it. And his friends would have never known it — because it would have been present within him inactive and dormant.

Likewise, no one will ever know that the healing power was given to you if you do not follow the same instructions to meditate and give yourself wholly to it. If you neglect it by never *thinking* about its presence, by never *talking* about its presence, and by never giving *thanks* for it, no one will ever know that the healing power was given to you when hands were laid on you. Your body will never know it, your family will never know it, your doctor will never be aware of it, and your friends will never realize it.

If the healing power is valuable enough for God to supply it to us through the sacrifice of His Son, then it is valuable enough to be *thought* about, *talked* about, and *thanked* about to keep it active in your life so that all can see what your Heavenly Father has given to you through the laying on of hands. *What you have given yourself wholly to will eventually appear unto all!*

I know individuals who have given themselves wholly to body-building, and it has definitely appeared unto all! Their body is a perfect display of the different muscle groups. When that person first began body-building, what he had given himself to wholly did not automatically appear unto all. But as time passed and he continued to give himself to body-building, it eventually became very evident that he had given himself wholly to body-building.

The person who receives his full healing manifestation is the person who has kept that power active within him by giving himself wholly to it. He refused to quit just because results did not appear instantly. *He stayed with it and kept the power working until he was satisfied with the fruit produced!*

So remember to *think*, *talk*, and give *thanks* to keep the healing power of God working within you!

# 11 chapter

## Law Number Eight:
Once the Power Has
Been Obtained, 'Keep
The Switch of Faith
Turned On'

As I mentioned in Chapter 10, for years I've heard Rev. Kenneth E. Hagin say things when he is ministering to the sick, such as, "The moment I lay hands on you, the healing power of God will be administered to your body. But what you do with it after that is up to you." And then he will say something else that's very interesting. He'll say, "Keep the switch of faith turned on."

Do you see that it is faith that not only *obtains* the healing power, but it is also faith that *keeps* the power working in us once it is obtained?

*Keep the switch of faith turned on!* Even though I have heard and used this phrase for years, I did not always fully understand what it meant. I had personally instructed people to keep the switch of faith turned on after I had laid hands upon them. But after a time, I found myself asking, "What does it really mean to keep the switch of faith turned on?"

I would ask others to define this phrase. They would tell me that it meant to keep believing. Well, that settled my heart for a while, so after I would lay hands on folks, I would tell them, "Keep believing." But then I began to ask the question, "Believe *what*? What exactly are we to believe?"

> *First of all, do you understand that we should not be telling people to "keep the switch of faith turned on" until we first determine if they even have the switch of faith.*

When we mention the switch of faith, are we talking about believing that God has raised Jesus from the dead? Are we talking about believing that God will provide for all of our needs? What are we talking about when we use this phrase "Keep the switch of faith turned on"? If we are unsure as to what we are to believe, then how are we to know that we have the switch turned on? It's hard to keep the switch of faith turned on if we are unsure as to what the switch of faith is.

## What Is 'the Switch of Faith'?

In pursuing the definition of "the switch of faith," I came across something that Rev. Kenneth E. Hagin said when he was speaking about the first time he ever used this phrase. As I listened to his story, he plainly gave the definition. I found out that the switch of faith is not just believing. Rather, it is a very *specific* belief. I am going to give you the story that Brother Hagin tells of the first time he used the phrase. He used it to help a couple who had a little child with clubbed feet. This is such a wonderful story — I trust that it blesses you as much as I have been blessed by it.

Brother Hagin was holding a meeting in a certain denominational church in which the people had received the baptism of the Holy Ghost and had gone charismatic. Several hundred of them had received this experience, and while Brother Hagin was there for eight days, another 150 were baptized in the Holy Ghost and spoke with other tongues. He also laid hands on the sick each night for healing.

One particular night, he was laying hands on the sick, and a young couple brought their only child, a little boy, to be prayed for. Both of his feet were clubbed feet; they were deformed. Brother Hagin held those little feet in his hands and ministered God's healing power to them. After doing so, he opened his eyes, looked at those little feet, and they were just as crippled as they were to begin with.

Brother Hagin said to the parents, in effect, "If it will help you any, I'll tell you this: I have a stronger anointing right now to minister to this boy than I have had with others in this prayer line before him. I'm just going to hold these little feet in my hands for a few minutes."

After a moment of holding those little feet in his hands, he opened his hands and looked at them again, and they were just as crippled and deformed as they ever were. So he said to them, "If it will help you any, I felt that power go right out of my hands into this child's feet." And then he said to them, "Keep the switch of faith turned on. Every time you think of it, say, 'The healing power of God has been ministered to those feet, and it's working in them right now.'"

Several weeks later, Brother Hagin was ministering in Tulsa. While he was ministering there, the son of the pastor of that denominational church, who was attending the meeting in Tulsa, got up to give the testimony of the couple with the little boy. He said that the young couple came back to his dad's church a few weeks after the little boy was prayed for and asked to show the child and to testify. With the pastor's permission, they brought the child up to the front of the church, and both of his feet were perfectly healed! Both feet were normal!

This was their testimony: "We did just what Brother Hagin told us to do. Every time we would look at those feet, we would say, 'Thank God the healing power of God was ministered last Thursday night to our child's feet, and that power is working in these feet now to effect a healing and a cure.' We did that every time we thought of it for three days and nights, and after the third day, the feet began to change. Little by little, they changed until they were just as perfect as feet could be!"

Glory! What a testimony! But the thing I want you to see is the definition of the switch of faith. Notice what Brother Hagin said to this couple: "Keep the switch of faith turned on. Every time you think of it, say, 'The healing power of God has been ministered to those feet, and it's working in them right now.'"

What is the switch of faith? It consists of two elements. The switch of faith is the belief that: (1) the healing power of God has been administered; and (2) the healing power is working mightily in your body to recover your body from the sickened condition.

As I became aware of this, a number of thoughts came to my attention. First of all, do you understand that we should not be telling people to "keep the switch of faith turned on" until we first determine if they even *have* the switch of faith. It's impossible to keep something *on* that you do not *have*. For example, I can't keep a flashlight on if I don't have a flashlight. So if I do not have the switch of faith, I can't keep it on.

We judge whether or not a person has the switch of faith by determining what the person believes in two areas: (1) Do they believe that the healing power was given to them when they were prayed for? and (2) Do they believe that the power is working in them now to drive out the sickness and disease?

> *Keep the switch of faith turned on! Every time you think of it, say, "I believe the healing power is working mightily."*

If they do not believe that the power is in them, then they do not have the switch of faith, and there is no reason to encourage them to keep it on. Likewise, if they do not believe that the power is in them working mightily to drive out the sickness, then they do not have the switch of faith, and there is no reason to encourage them to keep it on.

I am convinced that most people do not have the switch of faith. Why? Because they are in every prayer line that is offered to them. They are still trying to *get* God to heal them. They are still wondering whether or not they will ever be healed.

But remember the couple who brought the little boy to be ministered to by Brother Hagin? They believed that the power was administered to those feet, and they believed that the power was working mightily in those feet. And every time they *thought* of it they *said*, "Thank God, the healing power of God was ministered last Thursday night to our child's feet, and that power is working in those feet now to effect a healing and a cure!"

## Confession Keeps the Healing Power Active

This couple's confession of what they believed kept that power active and working until, after three days, the feet started changing. If they had stopped believing after *two* days that the power was in those feet, do you understand that they would have caused the power to become dormant or inactive, and their child's feet would continue to remain as they were? *Their loyalty to their belief that the healing power was administered, and their confession of what they believed kept the power working.* If they had stopped believing and confessing that the power was in their child's feet and working mightily, the power would have become dormant. They did the things that kept the power that was given by the laying on of hands active, not dormant. What were these things? *Thinking, talking,* and *thanking*!

Once you have been prayed for, from that moment on, you should be believing and talking about the healing power of God that is in you. As you do, all worry and fear will be dealt with.

I will use a natural illustration to "drive home" my point. Let's say you have a plant, and you haven't watered it in days. The plant is looking a little wilted. You are well aware of the fact that if no one puts water onto the plant, the plant will die. So you draw a glass of water and pour it onto the plant. Does the plant immediately jump to life? No. But all worry and fear that the plant is going to die is erased because you know that the water was administered and is working mightily to recover the plant. A few hours later, you walk by that plant, and it still looks as bad as it did before you watered it. But you go your way without a concern, knowing that the water is working mightily to recover the plant.

So it is with the healing power of God. When you are prayed for, the power is administered, and from that moment on, you can relax, knowing that the power is working mightily in you. Every time you think of it, you can lift your hands and say with a voice of confidence, "Thank You, Heavenly Father, that the healing power of God is in me mightily driving out the sickness and disease." *Think, talk,* and *thank*!

### Thanksgiving Is the Best Tool To Keep You in Remembrance of the Healing Power

The best vehicle to keep you thinking and talking about the power that was administered to you is thanksgiving. When you spend time giving thanks, you are putting yourself in remembrance of what God has done for you: "Thank You, Father, that power was administered to my body. I am not trying to *get* You to move; You have already moved on my behalf. Thank You that the power was given to me through the laying on of hands. It is working mightily in me. I can't feel it, but, Father, You said in Your Word that believers shall lay hands on the sick, and the sick shall recover. I believe that I am recovering. I want to thank You, Father, that if it wasn't for You — if it wasn't for the laying on of hands and Your power — I would remain sick. But now I believe that I am recovering."

Keep the switch of faith turned on! Every time you think of it, say, "I believe the healing power is working mightily." Before you take your medication, say, "Thank You, Lord, that Your power is working mightily in my body. Therefore, I believe that I am recovering." Every time you go to the doctor and he happens to give you a negative report, just say thank you and walk back to your car, shut the door, and say, "But I believe the healing power of God is in me, working mightily"!

(I encourage you to continue following your doctor's instructions, and keep taking your medication. But every time you take your medication, say, "The healing power of God is in me, working mightily. Thank You, Father!")

### Another Example of the Power of Thinking, Talking, and Giving Thanks!

After I became aware of these truths, I came in contact with a young lady who had not been able to keep food down for about six months. She had gone to medical doctors, and they had located a cancerous tumor in her stomach. In order to keep food down, she had to take medication before she ate each meal, so she began coming to some of my meetings for help.

After about two weeks, at the end of one of my lessons, I encouraged everyone to spend a little time worshipping God before I dismissed the group. As we began to worship God, I felt impressed to go to her and lay my hands on her and command that tumor to dry up and wither away in the Name of Jesus. When I did, I felt nothing go from me to her. We rejoiced a little more, and I dismissed the service.

The next day she came into the meeting "all smiles." She testified that after the previous day's service, she had gone to a restaurant with some friends and began to fellowship. Forgetting to take her medication, she ate, and after a couple of hours, she suddenly remembered that she had eaten and kept the food down without taking the medication! That night she purposely did not take her medication and ate her dinner. Again, she was able to keep the food down. As we heard her tell this wonderful news, we all rejoiced, and I said to her, "Now you keep coming to these meetings. Don't stop yet. Keep the switch of faith turned on." So she kept coming faithfully, smiling from ear to ear each day.

About three weeks later, she asked permission to speak with me after the teaching session. Now remember, I was teaching on healing every day. After the session, she asked me the question, "Doug, what would happen if I went back to the doctor, and he said that the tumor was still there and that cancer cells still exist throughout my bloodstream?"

Now I personally don't remember my response to her, but later she told me that all I said was, "So what!" and walked away.

The next day she came to me and asked the exact same question: "Doug, what would happen if I went back to the doctor, and he said that the tumor was still there and that cancer cells exist throughout my bloodstream?" This time I said to her, "Wait a minute. Do you believe that the healing power of God was administered to your body when hands were laid on you?"

She said, "Yes!"

I said, "Do you believe that the healing power is in you now, recovering you from this disease?"

Again she answered, "Yes!"

I said to her, "Then what difference does it make? If you believe that the healing power is in you and working mightily, then stick with what you believe."

The next day she came back and began asking the very same question she had asked the past two days in a row. Right in the middle of her question, I stopped her and said, "Wait a minute. What's going on?" She started to cry, and through the tears, she said, "Doug, what you don't know is that three days ago, I went to the doctor, and he said that the tumor is still there. He did say that it has shrunk a little, but it's still about a three-pound tumor, and the cancer cells are throughout my entire bloodstream."

"Just stick with what you believe," I encouraged her. "Every time you think of it, say, 'The healing power of God is in my body, and it's working in me to drive out the cancer. Thank God, I believe that I am recovering.'"

She dried up her tears, and for the next two weeks, she faithfully attended each session. Then I noticed one Thursday that she was not present in the healing class. Friday came and went, and she was still not in class. I told one of my workers that if she didn't show up the following Monday that we would contact her to see how things were going.

On Monday, I walked into the meeting, and there she was, "all smiles." She was jumping all over the place!

Finally, I got her to calm down and tell me the news. She said that on the past Thursday, her family had insisted that she have the tumor removed whether she could keep food down or not. They persuaded her to go to the hospital, and the doctors were ready to operate. But before they were to operate on Friday, they wanted to take another X-ray on Thursday. After the X-ray was taken and read, the doctors came to her and said that to their amazement, the tumor was completely gone! They could not find the nearly three-pound tumor! (The last time I saw this young lady was almost a year after this wonderful event, and she is as healthy as she can be. Glory!)

Now we must ask ourselves the questions, "What would have happened if she would have stopped believing that the power was in her? What would have happened if she would have stopped believing that the power was working in her, driving out the tumor and cancer? What would have happened if she would have stopped talking about it and giving thanks for what was administered to her through the laying on of hands?"

I am convinced that, had she abandoned her beliefs, she would have turned off the switch of faith, and the healing power that had been administered to her would have become dormant. The recovery process would have been stopped, and things would have gotten much worse in her life.

## Don't Fall Short of Receiving Your Manifestation

What is the switch of faith? As I said, it consists of two elements. It is the belief that: (1) the healing power of God has been administered; and (2) the healing power is working mightily in your body to recover it from the sickened condition.

If you have received the healing power of God into your body, every time you think of it, say, "The healing power is in my body, and it's working mightily in me now to drive out the sickness and effect a healing and a cure." It does not matter what you see or feel. Refuse to walk by sight, and choose to walk by faith.

Now you must understand that your ability to stay with what you believe determines the outcome. Should we yield to what our bodies are telling us or yield to what we see, we will be led into certain failure. If we do find ourselves abandoning our beliefs due to the circumstances we are facing, there is a scripture we can run to for help, and that is First John 1:9: *"If we confess our sins, he is faithful and just to forgive us our sins, and to cleanse us from all unrighteousness."*

The moment you find yourself governed by what you see and not by what you believe, ask the Father to forgive you and to help you arouse from dormancy the power within you. Say with boldness, "Thank You, Father. I believe that the healing power is in my body, and it is working mightily in me to effect a healing and a cure. I believe that I am recovering. I believe what Mark 16:17 and 18 says: '*And these signs shall follow them that believe; In my name shall they cast out devils; they shall speak with new tongues; They shall take up serpents; and if they drink any deadly thing, it shall not hurt them; they shall lay hands on the sick, and they shall recover.*'"

Keeping the switch of faith turned on teams *our* faith up with *His* power!

# 12
chapter

# What About Doctors?

So many today seem to have questions about the role of doctors in a Christian's life, especially when they are believing that the power is working in their bodies mightily. I cannot count the people I know of who have refused to see a doctor because they were afraid that if they knew what kind of disease they had, it might affect or weaken their faith.

I will never forget one lady who had a tumor that she could feel. After she told me what her situation was, my first response to her was, "Have you gone to a doctor to determine what you're up against?"

Her response was immediate: "No!"

I said, "Are you fighting the fear that this lump could be cancer and that you could die from it?"

She replied, "Every day I fight those thoughts."

I responded by informing her that she was fighting the fear of death based on no knowledge whatsoever. You see, when your mind does not know the facts, it will always come to the deepest, darkest conclusion that it could possibly think up. *Her fears were assumptions based on no facts whatsoever.*

I continued ministering to this lady by saying that one visit to the doctor could eliminate the fear of death by giving her understanding as to what the problem was and could, therefore, free her to place her attention on the real problem and not some dreamed-up fear. She finally agreed to go to a doctor, but she expressed another fear, which is also so common: She said that she was afraid that if she knew what the problem was that it might affect her faith and weaken it.

The moment she said that, the Lord gave me two illustrations to give to her. He showed me first that if knowing what you're up against would hinder your faith and weaken it, then He would have never counted the five thousand before He fed them! We find this account of Jesus' feeding the five thousand in Luke 9.

### LUKE 9:12-17

12 And when the day began to wear away, then came the twelve, and said unto him, Send the multitude away, that they may go into the towns and country round about, and lodge, and get victuals: for we are here in a desert place.

13 But he said unto them, Give ye them to eat. And they said, We have no more but five loaves and two fishes; except we should go and buy meat for all this people.

14 For they were about five thousand men. And he said to his disciples, MAKE THEM SIT DOWN BY FIFTIES IN A COMPANY.

15 And they did so, and made them all sit down.

16 Then he took the five loaves and the two fishes, and looking up to heaven, he blessed them, and brake, and gave to the disciples to set before the multitude.

17 And they did eat, and were all filled: and there was taken up of fragments that remained to them twelve baskets.

Notice the phrase ". . .*Make them sit down by fifties in a company*" (v. 14). Jesus knew how many were in the crowd before He began to feed them. And He told His disciples to count them too. So apparently, your faith doesn't have to be hindered or weakened by your knowing what circumstance you're up against.

Mark 11:23 is the second illustration the Lord showed me that will help us understand that knowing what we are up against will not affect or weaken our faith. In Mark 11, Jesus was teaching His disciples after they had witnessed the cursing of the fig tree.

He tells them in verse 23, "*For verily I say unto you, That whosoever shall say unto this mountain, Be thou removed, and be thou cast into the sea; and shall not doubt in his heart, but shall believe that those things which he saith shall come to pass; he shall have whatsoever he saith.*"

Jesus did not say, "That whosoever shall say unto *a* mountain." Notice Jesus used the words *"this* mountain," implying that He was pointing to a literal mountain. There must have been a mountain within view of the disciples when Jesus gave them this promise. If knowing what you are up against would affect or weaken your faith, I do not believe that Jesus would have pointed to a real mountain while giving this promise!

We must understand that knowing what we are up against will allow us to focus all of our attention on the problem and on the answer to the problem. It will aid us in ignoring imaginary problems and allow us to direct our faith to the problem. I encourage you if you are sick to find out what you are up against. Then follow your doctor's instructions, keep taking your medication, and above all else, *keep the switch of faith turned on*!